Unity and A Course in Miracles

Unity and A Course in Miracles

UNDERSTANDING THEIR COMMON
PATH TO SPIRITUAL AWAKENING

―∽―

William M. Heller & Paul Hasselbeck

Foreword by Reverend Stephen Colladay

Copyright © 2016 William M. Heller & Paul Hasselbeck
All rights reserved.

ISBN-13: 9781523938193
ISBN-10: 1523938196
Library of Congress Control Number: 2016906138
CreateSpace Independent Publishing Platform
North Charleston, South Carolina

Permissions

All quotes from *A Course in Miracles*© are from the Second Edition, published in 1992. They are used with written permission from the copyright holder and publisher, the Foundation for Inner Peace, P.O. Box 598, Mill Valley, CA 94942-0598, www.acim.org and info@acim.org.

All quotes and images used with permission of Unity School of Christianity, www.unity.org.

Dedication

This book is dedicated to all Unity and A Course in Miracles students, those committed to living these teachings and those who are curious.

Table of Contents

Foreword xiii
From the Authors xvii
Acknowledgments xxv
Introduction xxvii
How to Use This Book xxxi

Chapter 1   **Laying the Groundwork** 1
                The History of Unity and *A Course in Miracles* 2
                A Matter of Semantics 3
                A Birds-eye View of Unity and *A Course in Miracles* 4
                Summary 8

Chapter 2   **One Presence, One Power - What is and what is Not** 10
                Non-Duality 10
                Duality 14
                Different Language, Unified Message 16
                Duality and the Ego 19
                The Power of Mind 21
                Being in the World but not of It 23
                Summary 26

Chapter 3   **The Holy Trinity** 27
                Introduction 27
                God 29

	Terms used to Refer to God 30
	God is Spirit. 30
	God is Mind/Idea 32
	God is Creator. 34
	God is Love 35
	God is Cause or 1st Cause 36
	God is Father 37
	God is Principle. 37
	The Son of God, The Sonship, Christ 39
	The Holy Spirit 41
	Summary 44
Chapter 4	**Who is Jesus, Who am I?** 45
	Introduction 45
	Jesus, the Man 45
	Who am I? 47
	Our Current Perceived State 48
	Christ, Son of God, the Sonship 51
	Summary 53
Chapter 5	**Separation, Relative Mind and the Ego** 55
	Separation. 55
	Relative Mind. 58
	The Ego 62
	Summary 69
Chapter 6	**Specialness** 71
	Introduction 71
	All My Brothers Are Special 72
	Dreams of Specialness 74
	The Unholy Instant 74
	Specialness as a Strategy of the Ego 76
	Separation and Specialness 77
	Protection of Specialness. 79
	Special (Unholy) Relationships 80
	Special Hate (Unholy) Relationships. 84

	Special Love Relationships 85
	Summary 89
Chapter 7	**The Holy Instant, The Holy Relationship** 91
	Introduction 91
	The Holy Instant 92
	The Holy Spirit and Your "Special Function" 93
	The Holy Relationship 96
	Forgiveness and the Holy Relationship 99
Chapter 8	**Love and Fear, Sin, Guilt and Judgment** 102
	Love and Fear 102
	Sin and the Correction of Sin 105
	Correction of Sin (*A Course in Miracles*) 106
	Correction for Sin (Unity) 108
	Guilt 108
	Judgment 112
	The Last Judgment or Judgment Day 116
Chapter 9	**Healing Consciousness, Establishing Wholeness** 119
	Willingness 119
	Forgiveness and Repentance 121
	Miracles 124
	Conclusion (Miracles) 129
	Denials and Affirmations 129
	Denial (Unity) 132
	Affirmation (Unity) 132
	Denials and Affirmations are used together (Unity) 132
	Atonement 133
Chapter 10	**Concepts of the World and the Universe** 136
	Dream / Illusion 136
	The Physical Universe 139
	The Reason the Physical Universe Happened 141
	Time 145

	The "Real World" 147
	Heaven and the Universe. 149
Chapter 11	**The Physical Body, Sickness and Healing** 152
	A Course in Miracles. 153
	The Body 153
	The Source of Sickness 154
	The Body as a Tool of the Mind 155
	The Healing Process 156
	Unity. 158
	The Body 158
	Degeneration 159
	The Source of Sickness 160
	Generation 160
	The Healing Process 161
	Threefold Nature: Spirit-Soul-Body. 162
Chapter 12	**Unity's Twelve Powers** 166
	Christ 166
	Christ Consciousness. 167
	Developing Christ Consciousness – General 168
	Regeneration. 169
	Regeneration and the Twelve Powers 171
	How to Develop the Twelve Powers 173

Epilogue. 177
Bibliography and Resources 179
Authors' Short Biographies. 183
Endnotes:. 185

Foreword

By Reverend Stephen Colladay

IN 1982 WHEN I MOVED to Honolulu I almost simultaneously discovered two powerful spiritual teachings and paths that were destined to dramatically change my life, Unity and *A Course in Miracles*. I was deeply touched by Sunday services at Unity Church of Hawaii and Rev. David McClure's lessons and Unity principles which invited me to revisit and often reinterpret virtually all I had come to believe about Christianity, God, Jesus, the Bible, and myself. Who, me—a divine child of God, eternally loved and one with All That Is? Yes! And what a journey it has been.

Rev. David often referenced the Course in his lessons, and being on a roll of devouring one spiritual book after another, I naturally started attending David's classes on the Course and then weekly Course study groups.

As I grew in understanding their teachings of both Unity and the Course and applying them to my life, it was clear they were profoundly similar, even as they can and do stand on their own. My daily spiritual practice began to include both Unity and the Course material, and has continued for the past 34 years. When I was guided to ministerial school in 1990 there was no doubt that as a Unity minister, I would continue my personal practice and also integrate the Course in my Unity teachings. And so I did, and so I continue to do.

So it was with great delight and gratitude last month that I read Paul and Bill's *Unity and A Course in Miracles*. This book is a stellar, scholarly and accessible work that brings a new coherent understanding of the core teachings of these two important paths of Truth! Avoiding distracting grandiosity, the authors bring clarity to such areas, for example, as the similar but distinct language of the Fillmore's and Jesus in the Course; suggesting that "The Core premise underlying *A Course in Miracles* and Unity is non-dualism."

And this gem: "The most fundamental and underlying Truth found in both teachings is that God is our one and only Reality. They say we are an Idea in the Mind of God or God-Mind. It is a timeless, unchangeable Reality that can never be lost regardless of mistaken beliefs in separation and duality. Ultimately our journey or process is to undo these mistaken beliefs and to claim to Truth of our Divine Reality."

In 12 well written chapters, Paul and Bill offer straightforward insight to major Course and Unity teachings: The History of Unity and A Course in Miracles, One Presence, One Power, the Holy Trinity, Who is Jesus, Who am I, Separation, Relative Mind and the Ego, Specialness, The Holy Relationship, Real Relationship, Love and Fear, Sin, Guilt, and Judgment, The Process of Healing, Concepts of the World and the Universe, The Physical Body, Sickness and Healing, Unity's Twelve Powers, and Epilogue-Bringing it all Together.

I have not found any other source that offers the profound gifts offered by *Unity and A Course in Miracles--Understanding Their Common Path to Spiritual Awakening*. By shining their light of understanding and love of two transformational spiritual paths, Paul Hasselbeck and Bill Heller are to be thanked for walking the talk and sharing their profound work.

Unity and A Course in Miracles is a perfect resource for anyone wanting to create a dialogue and bridge between Course students and Unity students—which is the author's intention. I can envision a Course facilitator and a Unity minister, for example, jointly teaching a class or book study group using this text. The spirited discussion certainly would be awesome and, I believe, ultimately transformational for all.

In closing they say, "Ultimately, both teachings provide a path toward living from a higher state of Consciousness, through relinquishing thoughts of separation while embracing Oneness. What more could we ask? Thank you, Unity and *A Course in Miracles* for lighting our path." And thank you Paul and Bill for lighting *our* path!

Reverend Stephen Colladay

From the Authors

BILL'S STORY

Lao Tzu stated, "When the student is ready, the teacher will appear." This certainly applied to my journey into awakening to my spirituality through *A Course in Miracles* and Unity. As background, I left organized religion at age 15. Twenty five years later, in 1990, I had a "mountaintop experience," wherein I experienced love and peace like never before. This included a deep and profound love and acceptance of myself. Thus began an exploration to understand what happened on that mountaintop. A few months later, a friend asked me about spirituality in my life. While still absent, I was open to explore religion; I was open to learning about God after a long drought. So began a deeper inquiry into the Bible. Alas, over the next eight months, I found myself continuing to struggle with the Bible as in my earlier years. How did the Bible explain what I found in the world? Not at all; at least to my understanding.

During this same period, my experiences in life continued to unfold in a more positive and loving matter. New friends supported me in pursuing and accepting a more peaceful outlook of life. One new friend, George, gave me a most incredible line shortly after we met: "Well you know, Bill, there are only two emotions, Love and fear." My ride home that night was comprised of my looking at my life experiences, and sorting them out as either love or fear based. Little did I know how that was going to play in my life going forward.

William M. Heller & Paul Hasselbeck

Six months later, another friend suggested I read *A Course in Miracles*. When buying the book, I was asked if I wanted to look into a study group. "What for?" I wondered. Just the same, I jotted down some names and numbers of study groups. Those I called, no one returned a call. Instead, another friend pointed me to a class facilitator she knew, Randy Fuller. When contacting Randy, we spent a half-hour on the phone, the end of which he invited me to join his group. When completing the call, Randy made the statement, "Bill, I want you to know, before I asked you to join us, I was told to invite you." If I had heard this years earlier, I would have run in the opposite direction. Instead, this feeling, this experience, mirrored much of what I was now experiencing in my life.

When I first attended Randy's class, I knew I had found what I was looking for. Here were about 20 very bright students, both energetically and intellectually. They were two-thirds through the textbook at the time. While I could not fully comprehend what they were discussing, I could feel the energy, the enthusiasm, and the grace throughout the room.

So began an in depth study of "The Course" with Randy and his loving community over the next five years. Clearly, the teachings I found were fully describing what I was experiencing in my life, and providing even greater insights. I was developing a grasp of Jesus' message from 2000 years ago brought into a perspective that worked in my life.

Six months after beginning this study, some of my newfound friends invited me to visit the Unity Church in Palo Alto, California. I had heard some about Unity previously, and thought I should check it out sometime. I'd learned about the power of affirmative statements, and the "feel good" experience around Unity practitioners. With these new friends, I attended a service with over 400 people. Instantly, I was moved by the experience I felt—the energy, the smiles, the greetings all around, the lively music, and the heartfelt fire exuding from that day's visiting minister, Rev. Sallye Taylor. I'd never had such an experience in a church setting. Here was another wonderful community I felt energized by and grateful to find.

While I continued to explore other paths of spirituality, my experiences and connection with both Randy's community and the Unity

Unity and A Course in Miracles

community provided a deeper sense of connection and belonging—more so than ever before. While hearing some of the teachings of Unity, I also had a feeling of acceptance and belonging from a larger community than I'd ever had before. Early on, I appreciated more of the social contact I was finding in Unity. I'd say Unity was in the right place at the right time for me in this regard.

A year later, I began reading Charles Fillmore's (co-founder of Unity) books. Let me restate that- I began struggling through his writings wrestling with his writing style. At one point however that all changed. Reading Talks on Truth, I found Charles stating two key points now essential to my Spiritual trek: First, all of life stems from consciousness; God is Mind, and it's through our minds we are one with God. Secondly, the world I see is an illusion! The perception of the world I see stems through my mind, and thus is but a perception of my thoughts! This was the same message I was finding in my studies of *A Course in Miracles*! How exciting! Two sets of teachings were providing a different perspective of Jesus than I had learned early on in life. Further, following these teachings, I found my perspective on life was changing—wonderfully. The teachings were showing me the means of seeking and finding love and forgiveness in my life different than ever before.

I was hooked! While exploring different venues of new thought, spirituality, and physical healing of the body, Unity and *A Course in Miracles* were now the foundation for my spiritual perspective of life. The icing on the cake came a few years later when I took a Bible Study class through Unity. While I dreaded starting this class, and slipping into my previous resistance, the Bible came alive for me! I read of Peter and James hearing "Come along with me, and I'll make you a fisher of men." They dropped what they were doing, and joined Jesus. I was filled with so much compassion for them, and imagined what their experience must have been for them! In that moment, the Bible came alive for me. I recognized the means to read this was to look for the message of love in anything written there; also to question anything else as to its validity. This transition goes back to my first lines from George, "everything is based either on love or fear."

Clearly, I had found the teachings and the path were opening me to the message of love as our reality, and the means to experience God's Love throughout life. My life since the early 1990's has continued to affirm this path of love, this path of awakening.

My participation in both venues continued to expand—facilitating Course in Miracles Study groups, including an on-line workbook group, and growing involvement in the Course in Miracles Community. In Unity, I found the joy coming from classes, serving as a chaplain, and various leadership roles in both the Palo Alto and San Diego Unity communities.

In 2004, I realized my career in the corporate world was no longer sustainable. Support from my minister, Rev. Wendy Craig-Purcell, and my then current Course in Miracles guide, Bob Draper, led to my walking away from corporate finance, into my commitment to a spiritual life. I did not know what this would look like. In 2005, I realized the inner call I was feeling was to the Ministry—specifically, Unity. As wild as it seemed at that point, I was on fire; I'd never been so sure about my path going forward and certain as to the "next step" for me.

When applying to Unity's Ministry School, many advised me to "lay low" on my *Course in Miracles* involvement. I heard some about this dissension before; also, I learned it had been reduced considerably. This always puzzled me. One need only look at the two teachings together to find the essential universal truths both were offering, particularly the consistency in their means of offering the lessons of Oneness, healing, forgiveness, and our path of awakening.

For me to apply full out for a ministry program, it was important all knew the basis of my ministry lay in the integration of Unity and *A Course in Miracles* together. Gratefully, throughout the interview process, and subsequently throughout Ministry School, I was accepted into the fold.

About five months into Ministry School, I met Rev. Paul Hasselbeck. Paul was leading a "Metaphysical brown bag lunch" session providing an opportunity for us to compare notes about the metaphysics of both Unity and *A Course in Miracles*. I learned Paul was also as passionate about "The Course" being accepted and integrated into Unity's teachings. In 2007,

Paul and I discussed the possibility of a book to present the teachings of the two theological studies.

The rest is history. Since then, Paul and I have been compiling the material you now have in hand. I firmly believe this material will offer a means for Unity Students to understand the message of *A Course in Miracles*. The reverse holds true as well; I'm convinced students of the Course will be intrigued as they learn more about Unity. It's no accident so many Unity centers also offer *Course in Miracles* Study groups.

I also believe we offer material from Charles and Myrtle Fillmore that might be considered obscure or not fully understood. Personally, such material, presented in line with *A Course in Miracles* teachings are found to be more understandable.

William M. Heller & Paul Hasselbeck

Paul's Story

My first exposure to *A Course in Miracles* was not a "pretty one." In the early 1980s I was living in San Juan, Puerto Rico. Some of my friends and acquaintances began talking about *A Course in Miracles* – incessantly and with the fervor of an evangelist. My reaction to their demeanor was to run in the opposite direction. I got to the point where I actually avoided some of these people because that is all they could talk about. One of my closest friends gave me a copy and it promptly ended up on my bookshelf.

I eventually opened the text one day and began to read. I often did not know what it was saying but in some odd fashion it "rang true." I am not one to dabble at something. So, I jumped in with both feet and agreed to facilitate a group with my friend without knowing much about it. The best way to learn something is to be responsible for leading a group about it! I guess in some ways I became the one coming on with the fervor of an evangelist! The conversion of Saul from a persecutor of the Christians to a rabid evangelist for the Gospel comes to mind!

This group met for quite some time. It would grow and shrink. At one point we were squeezing 30 people into my friend's living room. We bonded very well as we studied together week after week. One friend, Raquel Olson, introduced the group to Tara Singh who we sponsored in Puerto Rico on several occasions. Another friend introduced us to the work of Dr. Kenneth Wapnick. This resulted in multiple trips to his center in Roscoe, New York.

After about two years, the group decided we wanted to have some sort of service on Sunday mornings and, yet, we were clear we did not want it to be focused on or from *A Course in Miracles*. We were strong believers in it being a self-study thing and not a church thing. We had heard there was a local church that sponsored Spanish *A Course in Miracles* groups. The minister there, Rev. Norma Rosado, agreed to start having services in English for us. This was my first introduction to Unity. I instantly saw a similarity in the teachings. Ironically, this became the only English Unity Church in Puerto Rico. I say ironically because here we were, founders of the only English Unity church without knowing much about it!

Unity and A Course in Miracles

This is not the place for me to go into my whole story. However, the short version is this. I was a practicing dentist in Puerto Rico. While treating a patient with AIDS I stuck an instrument into the palm of my hand. The patient died of AIDS two weeks later. I was diagnosed HIV+ 6 months later. I can authentically say I used the teachings of A Course in Miracles and Unity to meet this crises and to meet the illness head on. While I still carry the virus in my system I continue to thrive despite being told I would be dead in two years. That was 26 years ago!

I sold my dental practice and began volunteering for our budding Unity group. I also continued teaching and facilitating *A Course in Miracles* groups. I learned of Attitudinal Healing and began taking workshops with Center for Attitudinal Healing in Sausalito, California. I began leading several Attitudinal Healing groups. Eventually I learned how to train facilitators through the work of Dr. Susan Trout. This resulted in opening a Attitudinal Healing center in San Juan with my friend Annie Arbona. In October of 1993 I made a trip to Unity Village to study and check out what Unity believed at the World Headquarters. I learned some of the history between *A Course in Miracles* and the Unity movement. In the 1980s there was a warm and welcoming relationship between Unity and *A Course in Miracles*. However, at this point in time (early 1990s), *A Course in Miracles* was not exactly welcomed. During my month of study I clearly knew I was to apply to Unity's ministerial training. I applied and by July of 1994 I was beginning my ministerial training and was ordained in 1996.

It was during my ministerial training that I began advocating for a more welcoming attitude toward *A Course in Miracles*. I was peppering my comments and papers with quotes from *A Course in Miracles*. Eventually, one of the Vice Presidents became enthralled with "The Course" and even began teaching it on campus.

I also dug around the archives for information about the early relationship between *A Course in Miracles* and Unity. I found some promising titles in the archives - none of the materials did much for me. While titles seemed to promise a comparison between the two teachings, they did not deliver. I wanted a comparison between the two and eventually this became the seed impulse for me to join with Bill Heller to write this book.

William M. Heller & Paul Hasselbeck

I met Bill early in his ministerial training as a result of our interest in *A Course in Miracles*. We both desired a book that compared and contrasted the teachings while creating a bridge between the students of *A Course in Miracles* and the students of Unity. We met on nearly a weekly basis to brainstorm and write this book. We began meeting like this in 2007. While Bill was in school we met in my office. When he took a church assignment in Connecticut, we began meeting for two hours a week by phone. We decided Bill would be the "subject matter expert" for *A Course in Miracles* since I had not been actively reading it for over a decade. My area of passion is Unity metaphysics and I was serving as Dean of Spiritual Education an Enrichment for Unity Institute. Therefore, I was the Unity "subject matter expert." We chose topics to be explored in the book. Bill wrote the drafts based on *A Course in Miracles* and I wrote the drafts based on Unity's metaphysics. We then reviewed, commented upon and massaged each other's work until we got an agreeable piece of writing. The introduction to the topics were written in a variety of ways.

I can honestly say we were both practicing the teachings of *A Course in Miracles* and Unity as we co-created this book. I quickly learned writing a book with a co-author is not as easy as writing a book by myself! We had differing writing styles and, sometimes, differing points of view. Sometimes these were resolved rather easily while at least one topic, the ego, had us discussing our views for weeks on end. Eventually we did come to a satisfying agreement. I think we both thought we were finished a couple of times and then we would realize we had left out an important teaching. While we focus mainly on the similarities and how the teachings support each other, I think we did a good job of pointing out the distinctions as well.

I can honestly say this book is a labor of love. Love for *A Course in Miracles*, love for Unity and for Bill, my amazing co-author! You might wonder if this is simply another form of "specialness." I would answer yes and no! In this life, everything seems to start with specialness which then provides another opportunity for healing.

Acknowledgments

We are very grateful for the work of our editor and subject matter expert, Allen Watson. We are also grateful to Rev. Dr. Karrin Scapple, and Rev. Drs. Bil and Cher Holton.

We are also grateful to our teachers:

For Unity, ultimately, our gratitude goes to Charles and Myrtle Fillmore and then to the many Unity Ministers and Licensed Unity Teachers who have helped us along our way.

For A Course in Miracles, our gratitude ultimately goes to Helen Shucman, the scribe of *A Course in Miracles*.

Paul would like to thank: Dr. Gerald Jampolsky and the Attitudinal Healing Center in Sausalito, California, Dr. Susan Trout and especially Dr. Kenneth Wapnick, as well as, students and teachers in Puerto Rico – you know who you are.

Bill would like to thank: Bob Draper, Randy Fuller, Jon Mundy and Kenneth Wapnick. For all with whom I've studied these teachings, thank you! Gratefully I acknowledge your role in helping me understand these teachings.

Introduction

CONGRATULATIONS! SINCE YOU ARE EXPLORING this book you are demonstrating you are part of a continuing, upward spiraling stream of consciousness. There is ample evidence that human consciousness has been changing and growing over the millennia. In the late 1800's and early 1900s the spiritually-based New Thought movement arose and now includes several organizations: Unity, Divine Science and Religious Science. (While Christian Science excludes itself from New Thought, those who have studied both clearly understand that Christian Science played an important role in birthing the New Thought movement.) Over the decades New Thought has continued to grow and change as consciousness is continuing to grow and change. Many of the New Thought concepts have been verified by scientific research, and in turn, discoveries in the scientific world have resulted in changes in New Thought beliefs. In the opinion of the authors, *A Course in Miracles*, a spiritual teaching that arose in the midseventies, could be classified as a contemporary iteration of New Thought continuing this progression.

It is important to note that Unity, Divine Science, Religious Science and Christian Science have relied more upon centralized-organizational structures including the founding of churches and centers. *A Course in Miracles* has flourished without any single centralized-organizational structure; many independent organizations have arisen. Its dissemination has been more organic based upon the word of mouth and small study groups.

William M. Heller & Paul Hasselbeck

As ordained Unity Ministers, we know that Unity Teachings have grown and expanded as consciousness has grown and expanded since Unity's inception. Many of these teachings are more widely accepted and are more main stream today. Unity identifies itself as Christian based on its more contemporary New Thought perspective of the teachings of Jesus. Clearly, Unity's brand of Christianity differs from traditional Christianity in that Jesus Christ is not seen as uniquely divine. Unity teaches that each individual has innate divinity, the Christ. Jesus Christ is not the great exception. Jesus is the great example; Jesus Christ is our way shower. We believe and have experienced the power of the application of these teachings in our own lives. We experience greater peace and grace in our lives regardless of outer circumstances.

Eighty-five years following the formation of Unity, *A Course in Miracles* was first published. Beginning in 1965, Helen Schucman, Ph.D., began receiving inner dictation" of "The Course." A self-described atheist, raised in a Jewish family, Helen became convinced she was receiving this dictation from Jesus. William Thetford, Ph.D., Director of Clinical Psychology at Columbia-Presbyterian Hospital and Helen's supervisor, encouraged her in the "scribing" of "The Course" as it seemed to be the answer to their common desire to find a better way for people to interact with each other. Dr. Kenneth Wapnick assisted Dr. Helen Schucman in the final editing of the completed manuscript.

The Course is a self-contained, standalone teaching that was received as a unified whole. It is distinct from Unity where the teachings were compiled over an extended period of time from a variety of sources; Just the same, The Course complements and is consistent with Unity teachings. For this reason many Unity Truth Students add The Course to their daily studies. *A Course in Miracles* brings a new and fresh spiritual perspective to Unity, New Thought, and to all of humankind. It is a means to understand and amplify the teachings of Jesus Christ through a different perspective coupled with an effective daily practice.

Over the years there have been misunderstandings between both the Unity Community and the Course in Miracles Community. At one point in the past, *A Course in Miracles* was even banned by both Unity organizations. To a lesser extent there continue to be pockets of these misunderstandings. These detract from the commonality of purpose and message we find in both teachings.

Today, in many Unity Churches, teachings from The Course are now regularly integrated into Sunday Lessons. Both teachings advance and accelerate the attainment of the one goal: to forgive our errors in consciousness and to awaken to the Christ Mind.

This book is intended to bring these teachings together, as a means to advance and accelerate your journey of awakening. These teachings work hand in hand to awaken you to your Christ Nature, and to your eternal Oneness in God. Both teachings address information found in the Bible provided in a way that enables us to discover a workable application of Jesus' original teachings. These teachings demonstrate the divine power within us. They are a means of perceiving ourselves and this world in a different light in order to manifest the Christ potential within us. They also enable us to release the beliefs and judgments that have hindered us from knowing, applying, and experiencing the eternal truths of love, wholeness, and Oneness.

Let us be clear: This book compares the teachings of *A Course in Miracles* and Unity. It is not intended as a substitute for either learning *A Course in Miracles* or Unity. It is not intended to be the basis of the deep, heartfelt experience and insight one can attain by exploring and applying either one.

Come explore with us.

How to Use This Book

This book has no starting point or ending point even though we have put the topics in a sequence that makes sense to us. You may choose to read any topic at any time. The references for the Unity resources are very straightforward and follow conventional guidelines for such references. The references for *A Course in Miracles* proved more challenging as many editions of *A Course in Miracles* are available and in circulation.

Our understanding, research and presentation of the teachings of *A Course in Miracles* for this book utilizes the 1992 edition that was published by the Foundation for Inner Peace. This edition was based on the first edition that was authorized by Helen Schucman, Ph. D., the scribe of the original material. The original typing of Helen's notes by William Thetford, Ph. D., is not edited and not redacted and is now being published and disseminated as *A Course in Miracles, Urtext Manuscripts*. Reference to "The Urtext" material is NOT included in this book.

The following guide is intended to help the reader locate the references in *A Course in Miracles,*. The page numbers are used to reference material in the Course refers to the Second English edition published by the Foundation for Inner Peace in 1992.

The material for *A Course in Miracles* is included in three books: *The Text, The Workbook for Students, and The Manual for Teachers*. The Text provides the theoretical foundation for the teachings. The Workbook for Students is a series of daily lessons a student can use to apply the teachings and integrate its concepts into one's daily thought process. The *Manual for Teachers* (including the *Clarification of Terms*) provides more specific information about questions commonly asked about The Course.

Text, Workbook, Manual for Teachers and Clarification of Terms.

Text Text,
Example: (Text, 29.VI.1:3-5, pp. 615-616)
(Text Chapter 29, section VI, paragraph 1, sentences 3-5, pages 615-6)

Workbook Workbook,
Examples: (Workbook, P.I.83.3:1, p. 148)
(Workbook Part 1, lesson 83, paragraph 3, sentence 1, page 148)

(Workbook, P.II.12.331.2:1, p. 468)
Workbook, Part II Lesson 331, paragraph 2, sentence 1, page 468

Manual for Manual (Also Clarification of Terms)
Teacher

Examples: (Manual, 4.II.2:6-8, p.12)

(Manual for Teachers, Section 4, subsection II, Paragraph 2, sentences 6-8, page 12.)

(Manual, Clarification of Terms, 3.2:1-3, p. 83)
Manual for Teachers, Clarification of Terms, Section 3, paragraph 2, sentences 1-3, page 83.

CHAPTER 1

Laying the Groundwork

—⚅—

WE OFFER THIS BOOK AS the means to understand the common path to spiritual awakening found within Unity and *A Course in Miracles*. Their teachings differ from what has been offered through traditional Christianity. However, the essential concepts of both Unity and *A Course in Miracles* share common roots with traditional Christianity - the teachings of Jesus the Christ. Through experience and contemplation, Unity and The Course both offer a deeper and more contemporary understanding of Jesus' message, as derived through the continued evolution of our consciousness, and ability to comprehend his teachings in a different light.

Those of you who are Unity Truth Students are aware of the difference from traditional Christianity that brought you to Unity, and you have furthered your studies and spiritual development under these guidelines. The Fillmore teachings are basic, and over more than 120 years, Unity has further developed the message that the Fillmore's discovered and offered. We believe you have found such teachings work in your life, and provide you with a practical working sense of Jesus' message.

Students of *A Course in Miracles* have had the same experience through their studies: they are experiencing a greater sense of the love that Jesus the Christ had offered through his teaching. Gratefully, many of us who have studied both teachings have found the common thread between them, and are convinced that these teachings complement and even amplify one another.

Admittedly, this book can only present our own understanding of the teachings of *A Course in Miracles* and the teachings of Unity. Some of you may not agree with our understanding of either or both teachings. Ultimately, you, the reader must come to your own conclusion.

The History of Unity and *A Course in Miracles*

Does some sort of separation or "rift" exist within your Unity Community between those who study *A Course in Miracles* and those who identify themselves as Unity Truth students? Is there a perceived distinction between those who practice Unity Principles and those who study *A Course in Miracles*? Unity's relationship to *A Course in Miracles* (a spiritual teaching first published in 1975) has been most perplexing. Initially, The Course (*A Course in Miracles*) was well received within the Unity community. Many found this message a more likely description of Jesus' teachings than is found in traditional Christian churches.

Unity students who looked into these teachings found them to be congruent with Unity Basics, though more in content than in form. However, over time, some resistance arose to *A Course in Miracles* within the Unity community. It was even banned for a time from Unity bookstores because it was considered to be "channeled." Yet, many who have found Unity were also attracted to *A Course in Miracles*. Today, while there are still some Unity churches and centers that are not accepting of *A Course in Miracles*, many Unity Communities offer *A Course in Miracles* study groups. In fact, Unity Sunday Lessons are often sprinkled with quotes and concepts from *A Course in Miracles*.

Even so, in many Unity churches and centers, *A Course in Miracles* students and Unity Truth students do not intermingle much. This "separation" or "rift" may exist because of the mistaken belief that one method must be correct, right or better while the other is wrong or "less than" in some way. This separation is not necessary. Addressing these perceived differences is the reason we have written this book.

This type of separation is a form of what The Course calls "special relationships," a worldly concept where one person or belief must be correct at the expense of another. This type of separation is particularly ironic in A Course in Miracles community where the central message is one of practicing forgiveness to *end* separation and to heal relationships. The disharmony that arises from this perceived conflict between two belief systems can actually detract from the individual spiritual journeys of everyone involved. It blocks their realization of a deeper common Truth: their awareness of their own shared Divinity. Eliminating the conflict is a way of practicing forgiveness and healing the relationships that are involved.

A Matter of Semantics

Admittedly, the two teachings use different words to express their thoughts, perpetuating a belief that the teachings are different. However, these differences can actually serve to bring greater clarity to both teachings. When truly understood, these semantic differences fulfill a deeper purpose--we can use them to point the way to the change in consciousness we have longed for; a greater faith and understanding of God, Absolute Oneness as our True Reality.

For example, let's consider the term, *miracles*. Leading teachers of Unity, including Charles Fillmore, have stated "There are no miracles." Charles Fillmore states:

> There are no miracles in science. Jesus did no miracles. All His marvelous works were done under laws that we may learn and use as He did.[1]

Yet *A Course in Miracles* continuously refers to miracles; their application is an underlying principle to our awakening. In the "Principles of Miracles," we find many examples of their meaning within "The Course." For example:

> Miracles honor you because you are loveable. They dispel illusions about yourself and perceive the light in you. They thus atone for your errors by freeing you from your nightmares. By releasing your mind from the imprisonment of your illusions, they restore your sanity.[2]

> A miracle is a correction introduced into false thinking by me [Jesus]. It acts as a catalyst, breaking up erroneous perception and reorganizing it properly.[3]

Many other statements in this section refer to the miracle as a correction in our minds, moving our thoughts and beliefs to a higher consciousness, towards true spiritual awareness.

The difference in the way the two teachings use the word is this: Unity's statement addresses the traditional concept of miracle that seems to relate to a change in a physical condition; *A Course in Miracles* sees a miracle as a change in consciousness that can lead to a corresponding shift in one's physical circumstances. Both teachings emphasize that all healing occurs through moving one's mind to a higher consciousness of oneself; their means of describing this differs only in wording.

A statement in the *Workbook for Students* addresses miracles in a manner more consistent with Unity's statement of "awareness of a higher law:"

> And thus it [a miracle] illustrates the law of truth the world does not obey, because it [our worldly view] fails to understand its [miracle] ways.[4]

Throughout our book you will find discussions about differences in semantics. We believe identifying and addressing these will provide a bridge between the two teachings, showing their means to direct readers towards the higher goal of Spiritual Awareness.

A Birds-eye View of Unity and *A Course in Miracles*

The teachings of *A Course in Miracles* and Unity teachings are very compatible. In fact, we believe they are not only similar but in many ways identical. *A Course in Miracles* and Unity share the same overall objective – realizing Divine Mind, or Christ Consciousness, as the True Reality. They differ more in emphasis than in substance. *A Course in Miracles* focuses on undoing the belief in our ego-based thought system, thereby opening our mind to Divine Mind, or Christ Consciousness. Unity's focus is on realizing Divine Mind, and learning to choose the corresponding thinking over the ego, or worldly based thinking we have been used to. You will find more on this discussion throughout our material.

Charles Fillmore recognized the distinction between Absolute Truth and relative consciousness (sense and race consciousness); *A Course in Miracles* recognizes this as the distinction between Knowledge (God's Knowledge) and the ego-based perceptions of we use in our everyday lives. Both teachings focus on relinquishing relative consciousness/ ego-based perception by choosing to know and rely on God/our Christ nature.

A good overall starting point is to consider the Five Basic Unity Principles, and how these are paralleled within *A Course in Miracles*. The following table compares the two:

	Unity Basic Principle	***A Course in Miracles***
Principles 1 and 2 Define True Reality		
1	God is absolute good, everywhere present.[5] The central proposition in the inspiration of Spirit is that God, or primal Cause, is good.[6] …God is Spirit, the principle of intelligence and life, everywhere present at all times.[7]	God is All in All in a very literal sense. All Being is in Him Who is all Being.[8] The laws of God work only for your good, and there are no other laws beside His.[9] He [God] is what your life is. Where you are He is. There is one life. That life you share with Him. Nothing can be apart from Him and live.[10]

	Unity Basic Principle	*A Course in Miracles*
2	Human beings have a spark of divinity within them, the Christ spirit within. Their very essence is of God, and therefore they are inherently good.[11] The Spirit is the divine center in man and is always in the Absolute; it does not become involved in effects but stands as the creative Cause of the absolute good.[12] The personal man Jesus is merely the veil or mask worn by the spiritual man Christ or Jehovah. We are all, in our personality, wearing the mask that conceals the real, the spiritual, I AM. Jesus shattered that mask and revealed the spiritual man.[13]	Seek Him within you who is Christ in you.[14] Deep in your mind the holy Christ in you is waiting your acknowledgment as you.[15] "The name of Jesus is the name of one who was a man but saw the face of Christ in all his brothers and remembered God. So he became identified with Christ, a man no longer, but at one with God. ... In his complete identification with the Christ- the perfect Son of God, His one creation and His happiness, forever like Himself and one with Him - Jesus became what all of you must be.[16]
	Principles 3 – 5 are practices	
3	Human beings create their experiences by the activity of their thinking. Everything in the manifest realm has its beginning in thought.[17]	All thinking produces form at some level.[20] Projection makes perception. The world you see is what you gave it, nothing more than that. But though it is not more than that, it is not less. Therefore, to you it is important. It is the witness to your state of mind, the outside picture of an inward condition. As a man thinketh, so does he perceive.[21]

	Unity Basic Principle	A Course in Miracles
	Thought--A product of thinking; a mental vibration or impulse. Each thought is an identity that has a central ego, around which all its elements revolve. Thoughts are capable of expressing themselves. Every thought clothes itself in a life form according to the character given it by the thinker. The form is simply the conclusion of the thought.[18] The law of mind action will bring to pass what man believes in and expects.[19]	Whatever [thoughts] you accept into your mind has reality for you. It is your acceptance of it that makes it real.[22] What you project or extend [from your mind] is real for you. This is an immutable law of the mind in this world as well as in the Kingdom.[23] This is salvation's keynote: What I see reflects a process in my mind, which starts with my idea of what I want. From there, the mind makes up an image of the thing the mind desires, judges valuable, and therefore seeks to find. These images are then projected outward, looked upon, esteemed as real and guarded as one's own.[24]
4	Prayer is creative thinking that heightens the connection with God Mind and therefore brings forth wisdom, healing, prosperity, and everything good.[25] Prayer is the most highly accelerated mind action known. It steps up mental action until man's consciousness synchronizes with the Christ Mind. It is the language of spirituality; when developed it makes man master in the realm of creative ideas.[26]	Prayer is the medium of miracles. It is a means of communication of the created with the Creator. Through prayer love is received, and through miracles love is expressed.[28] The Bible emphasizes that all prayer is answered, and this is indeed true. The very fact that the Holy Spirit has been asked for anything will ensure a response.[29]

	Unity Basic Principle	*A Course in Miracles*
	We must pray, believing that we have received and we shall receive.[27]	True prayer must avoid the pitfall of asking to entreat. Ask, rather, to receive what is already given; to accept what is already there.[30]
5	Knowing and understanding the laws of life, also called Truth, are not enough. A person must also live the truth that he or she knows.[31] Each of us unfolds according to understanding and realization. Whether our understanding is little or great, we must demonstrate the Truth we know.[32]	A theoretical foundation such as the text provides is necessary as a framework to make the exercises in this workbook meaningful. Yet it is doing the exercises that will make the goal of the course possible.[33] Your mission is very simple. You are asked to live so as to demonstrate that you are not an ego.[34] This is not a course in the play of ideas, but in their practical application.[35]

Statements 1 and 2 define the nature of Reality; 3-5 are the practices to awaken or move towards a higher conscious awareness of our eternal Oneness with God. While the table shows the commonality of the two teachings, we will expand on this further as we provide deeper insights into the topical explanations of the two schools of thought.

Summary

The history of the relationship of *A Course in Miracles* and Unity certainly has ebbed and flowed. The Course has at times been accepted and other times shunned. Certainly, the language used in *A Course in Miracles* often differs from that found in Unity writings. This difference sometimes leads to misunderstanding. Fortunately, today, there is more of an accepting and welcoming attitude toward *A Course in Miracles* in the international organizations (Unity Worldwide Ministries and Unity World Headquarters at Unity Village) as well as in individual churches and centers. When the five basic principles of Unity are compared to teachings found in *A Course in Miracles* the similarity is quite obvious.

CHAPTER 2

One Presence, One Power
What is and what is Not

―⋘―

NON-DUALITY

THE CONCEPTS OF DUALITY AND non-duality are important when considering the teachings of Unity and *A Course in Miracles*. Non-Duality asserts there is no separation from God. This is the nature of our True Reality. Unity and *A Course in Miracles* both try to teach us this Truth, and to bring this Truth into our daily lives.

The best description we found on non-duality is derived from the online site for Science and Non-duality:

> Nonduality is the philosophical, spiritual, and scientific understanding of non-separation and fundamental intrinsic oneness. For thousands of years, through deep inner inquiry, philosophers and sages have come to the realization that there is only one substance and we are therefore all part of it. This substance can be called Awareness, Consciousness, Spirit, Advaita, Brahman, Tao, Nirvana or even God. It is constant, ever present, unchangeable and is the essence of all existence.[36]

This definition is essentially the basic view of both Unity and *A Course in Miracles*. It is predominant in Eastern Philosophies and Christian Mysticism.

Many Unity churches open their Sunday Service with a variation of this non-dualistic affirmative statement: "There is only One Presence and One Power active in the universe and in my life, God the Good, Omnipotence." Many people consider this from the perspective of theological, dualistic systems in which they were raised. To them it says something akin to, "There is only One Presence and One Power active in the Universe and in my Life, God the Good, Omnipotence," and, I am not God. I am something different and separate from God.'

When we believe there is God and our separate selves, we are in a dualistic belief system. Dualistic thinking is prevalent in our world. By definition, One Presence, One Power means non-dualism- there is nothing that is Real that is not God. Many are able to intellectually claim and understand the concept of "One Presence and One Power," but are unable to carry this awareness into their everyday lives. The deep and profound implication of this simple statement is everyone is the Oneness, commonly called "One with God."

We find references to non-dualism in the Bible. Many people believe Jesus awakened to the awareness of the Christ Mind (the Oneness) as his True Reality; he knew this as his Truth and as our Truth. The writer of the Gospel of John reports that Jesus stated, "The Father and I are one" (John 10:30, NRSV). The same writer reported Jesus' statement, "...I am in my Father, and you in me, and I in you" (John 14:20, NRSV).

A Course in Miracles

The following quotes demonstrate the stance on non-dualism that is presented in *A Course in Miracles*.

> The first in time means nothing, but the First in eternity is God the Father, Who is both First and One. Beyond the First there is no other, for there is no order, no second or third, and nothing but the First.[37]

While the first sentence sets up the second, it is the second sentence in which we are most interested. This sentence asserts there is only God. If that is true then we must assume our True Nature is God.

Here, *A Course in Miracles* is speaking to the omnipresence of God.

> There is no time, no place, no state where God is absent.[38]

And here we have a statement of non-dualism. What comes from God is God.

> All things that come from God are one. They come from Oneness, and must be received as one.[39]

This does not include the physical universe or the physical body because in our Oneness, these are illusions and unreal. Please see Chapter 10, Concepts of the World and the Universe. Here are more quotes on non-dualism:

> Heaven is not a place nor a condition. It is merely an awareness of perfect oneness, and the knowledge that there is nothing else; nothing outside this oneness, and nothing else within.[40]

> You are God's Son, one Self, with one Creator and one goal; to bring awareness of this oneness to all minds, that true creation may extend the allness and the Unity of God.[41]

> The statement "God created man in his own image and likeness" needs reinterpretation. "Image" can be thought of as "thought" and "likeness" as "of a like quality." God did create spirit in His Own Thought and of a quality like to His Own. There is nothing else.[42]

> God is All in all in a very literal sense. All being is in Him Who is all Being. You are therefore in Him since your being is His.[43]

> Nothing real can be threatened. Nothing unreal exists. Herein lies the peace of God.[44]

This final quote clearly states the distinction between the Real and the unreal. To The Course, only what is eternal and unchanging is real. For instance:

> …appearances are shown to be unreal [because] they change.[45]

> Reality is changeless. Miracles but show what you have interposed between reality and your awareness is unreal, and does not interfere at all.[46]
>
> I [Jesus] have said that only what God creates or what you create with the same Will has any real existence.[47]

We are at peace when we stop getting upset or reacting to this seemingly dualistic world we live in. Only God is Real; our dualistic thought system and physical world are unreal.

UNITY

Here are quotes on non-duality from Myrtle and Charles Fillmore:

> God is All-Intelligence; there is but the one Mind and in reality there are no separate men and women. A full realization of this great Truth would do away with all selfishness, the cause of all the misery of earth. We must understand clearly that the real life of all men is identical with our own and that aside from the one life all is illusion; that all seeming differences in people are caused by selfishness or desire for something separate and apart from God, or our fellow men.[48]

In truth there is but one mind; in it all things exist. Accurately speaking, man does not have three minds, [conscious, sub-conscious, and super-conscious mind] nor does he have even one mind; but expresses the one Mind in a multitude of ways.[49]

God is Mind, and man made in the image and likeness of God is Mind, because there is but one Mind, and that the Mind of God.... This one and only Mind of God that we study is the only creator. It is that which originates all that is permanent; hence it is the source of all reality.[50]

There is no duality in God.[51]

In the serene mind of God there is no duality, no good-and-bad, and no understanding-and-ignorance. The brilliancy of all-knowing Mind dissolves all shadows, all negations.[52]

Duality

Duality is the consciousness of separation. Looking at the evidence provided by our senses it seems apparent that duality is the basis of the world in which we live. In our day to day lives, we certainly think and experience ourselves as separate from one another. One might say all the drama and excitement of life are based on this notion of duality and separation. This dualistic experience arises from the mistaken belief that I am or we are separate and different from God. Once we have accepted this belief in separation we seem to lose all access to the unchanging certainty of the Mind of God (Divine Mind). We have restricted our thinking to our individualized consciousness.

Duality includes ideas and perceptions of life that are based on "something is or is not." We use judgment to establish and maintain these polarities in our experience of life. In addition to God – not God / Real-not real polarities, other examples would be love-fear, right - wrong, better - worse, good-bad, and good-evil.

Once separation consciousness gets locked into our thinking, we believe we are alone, and believe our survival is dependent upon our limited selves. Such thinking is reflected in negative emotions and behavior—fear, judgment, error, the need to be right, the need to control, and the habit of making decisions that fail to take into account the Whole of Reality, God.

Both teachings assert that our True Nature/our True Reality is non-dualistic and what is real. Our senses and our beliefs are derived from the experience of separation in this physical realm. This separation consciousness is not real; both *A Course in Miracles* and Unity call separation unreal.

A Course in Miracles

From the *Glossary-Index of A Course in Miracles*, we find this description of separation.

> The belief in sin that affirms an identity separate from our Creator; seemed to happen once, and the thought system which arose from that idea is represented by the ego; results in a world of perception and form, of pain, suffering, and death, real in time, but unknown in eternity.[53]

And from *A Course in Miracles Text*:

> Separation is only the decision not to know yourself. This whole thought system is a carefully contrived learning experience, designed to lead away from truth and into fantasy.[54]

> The separation is merely a faulty formulation of reality [unreal], with no effect at all.[55]

> The instant the idea of separation entered the mind of God's Son, in that same instant was God's Answer given. In time this happened very long ago. In reality it never happened at all.[56]

Unity

From Unity, we find:

> Man is a duality in seeming only. He is a unit when he knows himself. His ignorance of himself and his relation to God is the cause of the seeming duality. When wisdom comes to him and he makes wisdom his own, there is no longer war between the ideal man in God and the becoming man in the Lord God.[57]
>
> The person in sense consciousness thinks he has a mind of his own and that he creates thought from its own inherent substance. This is a suppositional mind that passes away when the one and only real Mind is revealed. [58]
>
> Changes are constantly taking place and will continue so long as we live in the consciousness of duality, the "yes" and "no" state of existence, which is mortality.[59]

Truth not only shows the reality at the core of all things; it also shows that we shall never escape from the unreal so long as we allow our mental processes to clothe it with "thought stuff."[60]

Different Language, Unified Message

The two belief systems use different words to describe the distinction between Non-duality and duality, what is Real and unreal.

A Course in Miracles

Knowledge and Perception
In *A Course in Miracles*, "Knowledge is God" and it is what is real. It is changeless, limitless, and timeless.

Knowledge is truth, under one law, the law of love or God. Truth is unalterable, eternal and unambiguous. It can be unrecognized, but it cannot be changed. It applies to everything that God created, and only what He created is real.[61]

Early in the Text of *A Course in Miracles*, one entire section introduces the distinction between perception and Knowledge. Knowledge is described relative to perception, for the Knowledge of God is all that is Real and eternal, and anything that is not of God occurs through perception. Thus:

Knowledge is timeless, because certainty is not questionable.[62]

Knowledge is power because it is certain, and certainty is strength. Perception is temporary.[63]

The unreal is the world of perception in *A Course in Miracles*:

The world of perception, on the other hand, is a world of time, of change, of beginnings and endings. It is based on interpretation, not on facts. It is the world of birth and death, founded on the belief in scarcity, loss, separation, and death. It is learned rather than given, selective in its perceptual emphases, unstable in its functioning, and inaccurate in its interpretations.[64]

The world as you perceive it cannot have been created by the Father, for the world is not as you see it. God created only the eternal, and everything you see is perishable. Therefore, there must be another world that you do not see.[65]
 You see a world that you have made, but you do not see yourself as the image maker. You cannot be saved from the world, but you can escape from its cause. This is what salvation means, for where is the world you see when its cause is gone?[66]

The ego-based belief system arises from perception.

Unity

Absolute and Relative

The historical Unity writings describe the distinction between Non-duality and duality as the Absolute and the relative. The Absolute is Real and the relative is unreal. Over time these have come to be known as the Absolute Realm and the relative realm. The quotes used in this section will use the traditional Absolute and relative nomenclature.

Unity's Absolute realm is timeless, changeless and limitless. It is Omniscience, Omnipotence and Omnipresence. The Absolute is complete, the All. It is not measured by space or time. God, the Absolute, is not a "Who." God is "What." Some Unity based quotes follow:

> Absolute--Divine Mind; unlimited Principle; the almighty One; the all-pervading Spirit; the Infinite; the Eternal; the Supreme Being. The one ultimate creative Mind; the Source of all things. That which is unconditioned, unlimited, unrestricted, and free from all limitations. The self-existent God.[67]

> It is only from the plane of mind that one can know Truth in an absolute sense. ... the absolute Truth endures; and what is true today always was and always will be true.[68]

> Reality ["Reality"] --That which is abiding, eternal, and unchangeable, the same "yesterday and today, yay and forever" (Heb. 13:8).[69]

The relative and its sense-based consciousness always changes and is limited. It has its roots in ego-based beliefs developed and perpetuated in our individualized, ego-based perception of our lives and of the world around us. Beliefs actually are perceptions and are a manifestation of our separation/sense-based thinking. These beliefs develop from past experiences, thoughts and decisions made on our own or derived from beliefs we have accepted from others.

These beliefs are temporary and change due to our limited judgments of circumstances that are perceived in a moment. We then turn around and use these same sense-based beliefs/perceptions as a lens to perceive our life and the world around us. It is a seeming unending circle that began with the first belief in separation. Since beliefs are subject to change and/or release, they are not certain. As a result of this uncertainty, we doubt, we question, and we change; guilt and fear are some of the effects of the relative sense-based consciousness we live with.

> The relative truth is constantly changing …. [70]
> Mind. Mortal - … It is the opposite of the Christ Mind… Mortal mind gathers its information through the senses. It judges by appearances, which are often false judgments.[71]

> Sense consciousness--A mental state formed from believing in and acting through the senses. … Judgments based on outer appearances--the senses—produce discordant thoughts, jealousies, and a host of limiting beliefs.[72]

> Man's intellectual standards are determined according to the judgments of the senses.[73]

DUALITY AND THE EGO

The ego is an effect of the thought of separation; the ego continues to exist as long as we believe in separation. The unreal world of ego-based perceptions is changeable, limited, of time; it is temporary. This unreal world of separation consciousness is based on fear, guilt, judgment, competition, isolation and lack.

For the most part, our day to day activities rest on the notion of separation, making it difficult to relinquish duality in our thinking. Our lives, our world, and our bodies seem to be entirely focused in and from this state of duality. Since we are the ones "making up" the ego, we love and protect it.

A Course in Miracles

The ego arose from the separation, and its continued existence depends on your continuing belief in the separation. The ego must offer you some sort of reward for maintaining this belief. All it can offer is a sense of temporary existence, which begins with its own beginning and ends with its own ending.[74]

Consciousness is correctly identified as the domain of the ego. The ego is a wrong-minded attempt to perceive yourself as you wish to be, rather than as you are.[75]

No one dismisses something he considers part of himself. You react to your ego much as God does to His creations—with love, protection and charity. Your reactions to the self you made are not surprising. ... the question is not how you respond to the ego, but what you believe you are.[76]

You perceive the world and everything in it as meaningful in terms of ego goals. These goals have nothing to do with your own best interests, because the ego is not you.[77]

Unity

The personal self is the ego around which revolve all thoughts that bind us to error. We cannot cross all out at once, but little by little we cast out the specific thoughts that have accumulated and built up the false state of consciousness termed Judas. In the life of Jesus, Judas represents the false ego that error thought has generated.[78]

Personality – The sum total of characteristics that each person has personalized as distinct of himself, independent of others or of divine principle. ... Personality is what people seem to be when they thin in their three-dimensional consciousness; ...[79]

Ego, adverse--When the ego attaches itself to sense consciousness, it builds the antichrist man, who has no basis in reality. This is known as the adverse ego. It is the adverse ego that causes all the trouble in the world. Its selfishness and greed make men grovel in the mire of materiality, when they might soar in the heavens of spirituality.[80]

The Power of Mind

The Power of Mind is an important topic. Both teachings address Mind as the One Reality, God. Each points to the Creative aspect of God; we are an Idea in n the Mind of God. As God's creation, we have the full capability of God-Mind. Not being aware of our mind's True Capability has brought about both teachings.

We use the Power of the Mind to make a dualistic state. We believe we are limited in all aspects of life. This is an error. Both Teachings recognize that life occurs from our mind. The thoughts we have, extend and/or project manifest life as we perceive it.

A Course in Miracles

The oneness of the Creator and the creation is your wholeness, your sanity and your limitless power. This limitless power is God's gift to you, because it is what you are. If you dissociate your mind from it you are perceiving the most powerful force in the universe as if it were weak, because you do not believe you are part of it.[81]

Few appreciate the real power of the mind, and no one remains fully aware of it all the time. However, if you hope to spare yourself from fear there are some things you must realize, and realize fully. The mind is very powerful, and never loses its creative force. It never sleeps. Every instant it is creating. It is hard to recognize that thought and belief combine into a power surge that can literally move mountains.[82]

God created His Sons by extending His Thought, and retaining the extensions of His Thought in His Mind. All His Thoughts are thus perfectly united within themselves and with each other… God created you to create.[83]

UNITY

The ideas of God are potential forces waiting to be set in motion through proper formative vehicles. The thinking faculty in man is such a vehicle, and it is through this that the visible universe has existence. Man does not "create" anything if by this term is meant the producing of something from nothing; but he does make the formless up into form; or rather it is through his conscious co-operation that the one Mind forms its universe. Hence the importance of man's willing co-operation with God in every thought, because unless he is very wise in his thinking, he may be sending forth malformations that will cause both himself and the universe trouble. [84]

When the mind attains an understanding of certain creative facts, of man's creative powers, it has established a directive, intelligent center that harmonizes these two men (ideal and spiritual vs. intellectual and material). This directive center may be named the I AM. It is something more than the human I. Yet when this human

I has made union with the image-and-likeness I, the true I AM comes into action, and this is the Christ Jesus, the Son of God, evolved and made visible in creation according to divine law.[85]

Jesus said that a man would be held accountable for "every idle word," and a close observation of the power of mind in the affairs of the individual proves this to be true. What we think, we usually express in words; and our words bring about in our life and affairs whatever we put into them. A weak thought is followed by words of weakness. Through the law of expression and form, words of weakness change to weakness the character of everything that receives them. [86]

Being in the World but not of It

Non-Duality asserts there is no separation from God. This is the nature of our True Reality. Is it possible to view life through such a non-dualistic consciousness, while continuing life as we live it today? Unity and *A Course in Miracles* both assure us that it is possible, and try to teach us this Truth, and to bring this Truth into our daily lives by retraining our minds.

Divine Mind is the source from which we can formulate appropriate answers, solutions, or courses of action to any matter or situation. Consistently choosing non-dualism over dualism furthers our progress towards recognizing the "One Presence and One Power active in the Universe and in my Life; God the Good, Omnipotence."

A Course in Miracles

A Course in Miracles calls living from a non-dual consciousness living "in the real world." It describes the experience of "God's teachers," those living in the real world, in this beautiful passage:

"God's teachers choose to look on dreams a while. It is a conscious choice. For they have learned that all choices are made consciously, with full awareness of their consequences. The dream says otherwise, but who would put his faith in dreams once they are recognized for what they are? Awareness of dreaming is the real function of God's teachers. They watch the dream figures come and go, shift and change, suffer and die. Yet they are not deceived by what they see. They recognize that to behold a dream figure as sick and separate is no more real than to regard it as healthy and beautiful. Unity alone is not a thing of dreams. And it is this God's teachers acknowledge as behind the dream, beyond all seeming and yet surely theirs.[87]

Even though we have selected a few choice quotes from the text of *A Course in Miracles*, a few quotes do not do justice to the fact that the purpose of the entire workbook of *A Course in Miracles* is to retrain our minds.

The ego made the world as it perceives it, but the Holy Spirit [an aspect of Divine Mind], the reinterpreter of what the ego made, sees the world as a teaching device for bringing you home.[88]

There is no point in lamenting the world. There is no point in trying to change the world. ...it is merely an effect. But there is indeed a point in changing your thoughts about the world. Here you are changing the cause. The effect will change automatically.[89]

There is no world apart from what you wish, and herein lies your ultimate release. Change but your mind on what you want to see, and all the world must change accordingly.[90]

The images you make cannot prevail against what God Himself would have you be [Christ]. Be never fearful of temptation [separation thinking], then, but see it as it is; another chance to choose again, and let Christ's strength [our True Nature's strength] prevail in every circumstance and in every place you raised an image of yourself [ego] before.[91]

Later in this same section:

What you behold as sickness and pain, as weakness and as suffering and loss, is but temptation to perceive yourself defenseless and in hell. Yield not to this… Choose once again what you would have him [yourself or another] be [Christ], remembering that every choice you make establishes your own identity as you will see it and believe it is.[92]

UNITY

All that man manifests has its origin in a cause that we name Divine Mind. The one Mind is absolute …[93]

To get perfect results it is necessary to deal with our mind in both the absolute and the relative.[94]

By realizing the Mind of Christ, he [each person] becomes one with the Absolute.[95]

When man gets into the understanding of the Absolute, he takes his freedom from all bondage of time and declares that time shall no more enter into the substance of his mind or body or affairs.[96]

While seeming to live in the relative we can still utilize "What" [Christ Mind] we are in order to manage day-to-day living from a higher state of consciousness.

Summary

The core premise underlying both *A Course in Miracles* and Unity is non-dualism. All of the teachings and practices rely on this one concept; there is only One Power and One Presence, period. God is Real, unchanging, timeless and unlimited. Anything that is changing, of time or limited is unreal, an illusion, no matter how "real" they may seem to be according to our senses. The unreal arose from the error belief in separation that is based on fear, guilt, judgment, competition, isolation and lack. The "way back" occurs through re-training our consciousness based on the awareness of our True Realty, the Oneness Itself, and the correction of error thoughts and beliefs.

CHAPTER 3

The Holy Trinity

―⁂―

INTRODUCTION

BOTH *A COURSE IN MIRACLES* and Unity use the traditional Christian concept of the Trinity to explain and understand the Oneness of God. From the literature, it can be difficult to discern if the Unity writers and scribe of ACIM literally believe in the Trinity. However, it is clear that they made a concerted effort to interpret the Holy Trinity as a means to describe the nature of the Divine. This is entirely appropriate, given that the audience was probably aware of the concept of the Holy Trinity.

The doctrine of the Trinity was discussed beginning in the Second Century, and was formulated in its current form by the Council of Nicaea around 325 C.E. The best definition found was from Easton's Bible Dictionary:

> … a word not found in Scripture, but used to express the doctrine of the unity of God as subsisting in three distinct Persons. This word is derived from the Greek trias, first used by Theophilus (A.D. 168–183), or from the Latin. trinitas, first used by Tertullian (A.D. 220), to express this doctrine. The propositions involved in the doctrine are these: 1. That God is one, and that there is but one God (Deut. 6:4; 1 Kings 8:60; Isa. 44:6; Mark 12:29, 32; John 10:30). 2. That the Father is a distinct divine Person (hypostasis, subsistentia, persona, suppositum intellectuale), distinct from the Son and the Holy Spirit. 3. That Jesus Christ was truly God, and

yet was a Person distinct from the Father and the Holy Spirit. For that the Holy Spirit is also a distinct divine Person. [97]

A Course in Miracles

Throughout the text of *A Course in Miracles*, there are references to the Holy Trinity. In some of the descriptions of the existence of the Holy Trinity, its Oneness, or all-inclusive nature or function of each aspect is addressed:

> The Son of God is part of the Holy Trinity, but the Trinity Itself is one. There is no confusion within Its Levels, because They are of one Mind and one Will. This single purpose creates perfect integration and establishes the peace of God,[98]

> The Holy Trinity is holy because It is One. If you exclude yourself from this union, you are perceiving the Holy Trinity as separated. You must be included in it, because It is everything. Unless you take your place in It and fulfill your function as part of It, the Holy Trinity is bereft as you are. [99]

Unity

It would seem both Charles and Myrtle Fillmore believed in the Trinity given the language they used. However, clearly, both believed God to be Mind (God-Mind), Principle, and that God is not a person, being or entity. Charles Fillmore metaphysically interpreted the doctrine of the Trinity so as to make it useful to a metaphysical Christian.

> We are studying spiritual science to get a broader conception of God, rather than holding to the view that He is a personal being

with parts like a man, a being subject to change and capable of varying moods. Though personal to each one of us, God is *IT*, neither male nor female, but Principle… [100]

The Trinity is known commonly as Father, Son, and Holy Spirit; metaphysically it is known as mind, idea, expression. These three are one. Each sees itself as including the other two, yet in creation separate …

Reducing the Trinity to simple numbers takes away much of its mystery. When we say that there is one Being with three attitudes of mind, we have stated in plain terms all that is involved in the intricate theological doctrine of the Trinity.[101]

GOD

Both *A Course in Miracles* and Unity embrace a similar view of God, the Divine. While using very traditional language in reference to God, using pronouns like "He" or "Him," and anthropomorphic terms like Father and Creator, neither one supports a traditional view of God. God is not a person, entity or being. God is NOT a Being or the Being. God is Being (Beingness).

A Course in Miracles

The following quotes taken together make it clear that God is not a person, being or entity. Obviously, if God does not know form then God cannot be a form. Further, people, entities and beings are usually thought to have a personality (ego). The second quote clearly states that God does not have an ego with which to judge or to perceive.

God, Who encompasses all being…[102]

God knows not form. He cannot answer you in terms that have no meaning.... Creation gives no separate person and no separate thing the power to complete the Son of God.[103]

The Bible repeatedly states that you should praise God. This hardly means that you should tell Him how wonderful He is. He has no ego with which to accept such praise, and no perception with which to judge it.[104]

Unity

The Principle of Being is not only all good, but it is all intelligent. It is the fount of your intelligence.[105]

God is not a being or person having life, intelligence, love, power. God is that invisible, intangible, but very real, something we call life. God is perfect love and infinite power. God is the total of these, the total of all good, whether manifested or unexpressed.[106]

Terms used to Refer to God

The sections that follow address some of the terms both teachings use to describe God.

God is Spirit

A Course in Miracles

Please remember that the material in *A Course in Miracles* is directed towards the reader. It is written to the reader in relation to God; continuously emphasizing oneness. Thus, it is difficult to separate out the term spirit in relation to God and the term spirit in relation to the Son of God, Christ. In *A Course in Miracles*, The term "spirit" is given two different meanings. Spirit is referred to as God, and it is also referred to as God's Creation- the Son of God. These two different meanings actually enhance the material's essential teaching that God's creation is the expression of God, and fully included within, always.

God is with me…. the Spirit which directs my actions…[107]

It still remains within you…to extend as God extended His Spirit to you.[108]

God's teachers have God's Word behind their symbols. And He Himself gives to the words they use the power of His Spirit… [109]

Unity

God is Spirit, the Principle of creative life, the moving force in the universe, the omnipotent, omnipresent essence from which all things proceed.[110]

God is Spirit, or the creative energy that is the cause of all visible things. God as Spirit is the invisible life and intelligence underlying all physical things. There could be no body, or visible part, to anything unless there was first Spirit as creative cause.[111]

Spirit is not matter. Spirit is not person. In order to perceive the essence of Being we must drop from our mind all thought that God is in any way circumscribed or has any of the limitations that we associate with things or persons having form or shape." [112]

God is Mind/Idea

The Absolute (Knowledge), God, is both Mind and Idea. Since the Absolute is Oneness then Mind and Idea must be synonyms; each provides an opportunity to understand a facet of God. In a way, the One Idea is the One Mind.

A Course in Miracles

Many of the references to Mind use the phrase "Mind of God." This usage continues in the anthropomorphic language of *A Course in Miracles*. However, there is some indication that God is Mind and Idea.

> ...because you recognize, however dimly, that God is an idea...[113]

An Idea must exist in Mind (God Mind, or Mind of God).

> The term mind is used to represent the activating agent of spirit, supplying its creative energy. When the term is capitalized it refers to God or Christ.[114]
> God is the Mind with which I think.[115]

From the *Glossary-Index for A Course in Miracles*, we find the definition that follows. The emphasis here is there is but one Mind, and that is the Mind of God.

> Mind of God-equated with the creative function of God which represents the activating agent of spirit, supplying its creative energy;...[116]

> God's Mind cannot be lessened. It can only be increased, for everything He creates has the function of Creating.[117]

UNITY

God is Mind… there is but one Mind, and that the Mind of God.[118]

Divine Mind – God-Mind; ever-present, all-knowing Mind; the Absolute, the unlimited, Omnipresent, all-wise, all-loving, all-powerful Spirit.

There is but one Mind, and that Mind cannot be separated or divided, because, like the principle of mathematics, it is indivisible. All that we can say of the one Mind is that it is absolute and that all its manifestations are in essence like itself.[119]

… God Mind embraces all knowledge, wisdom, and understanding and is the source of every manifestation of true knowledge and intelligence.[120]

The creations of the one Mind are ideas. The ideas of God are potential forces waiting to be set in motion through proper formative vehicles [thoughts]. The thinking faculty in man is such a vehicle, and it is through this that the visible universe has existence.[121]

The law of manifestation for man is the law of thought. God ideates: man thinks. One is the completion of the other in mind.[122]

The previous quotes provide a clear delineation of Unity's teaching on "mind-idea-expression." The first sentence talks about the one Mind and Ideas. Next, the ideas are "waiting to be set in motion" by thoughts. Thoughts are of the relative realm as are the effects of thoughts upon Ideas. "Expression" is clearly of the relative realm and not the Absolute Realm of Divine Mind-Idea.

If we get the key to man's real being, which is mind and the activity of mind, we will immediately discern that we have within us those three activities of mind, the Father mind, the Son mind, and the Holy Spirit mind. In other words, the mind and the idea and the manifestation of the idea. These three come in every one of us. ... We have within us, every one of us, the key that unlocks the understanding of God. And that key is to know ourselves. ... the key for the Holy Spirit is in the activity of the executive power [the Power of Will] of man's mind. You know we base our thinking upon Mind and then the idea in Mind and then the manifestation or expression of the idea; in other words, the power of thought.[123]

God is Creator

A Course in Miracles

God as Creator is SO important in The Course; "I am as God created me" is reiterated over and over, and the separation is attributed to the insane idea that we can alter God's creation and create ourselves. If we truly grasp God as our Creator, the separation is entirely healed.

> He [God] is first in this sense that He is the First in the Holy Trinity Itself. He is the Prime Creator, because He created His co-creators. Because He did, time applies neither to Him nor what He created.[124]

> The Creator of life, the Source of everything that lives, the Father of the universe and of the universe of universes, and of everything that lies even beyond them would you remember.[125]

> What else but you did the Creator create, and what else but you is the Kingdom?[126]

In the creation, God extended Himself to His creations."[127]

...God created you by extending Himself as you...[128]

UNITY

God is Creator. We are creation. We exist or show forth our Creator. [129]

This one and only Mind of God that we study is the only creator. It is that which originates all that is permanent; hence it is the source of all [R]reality. [Divine ideas.][130]

God creates through the action of His mind, and all things rest on ideas. [131]

GOD IS LOVE

A COURSE IN MIRACLES

God is Love and you do want Him.[132]

The Love of God is in everything He created, for His Son is everywhere.[133]

God is but Love, and therefore so am I.[134]

UNITY

He that loveth not knoweth not God; for God is love.[135]

It is popularly taught and believed that there is but one love; that God is love and that all love is from Him, hence that all love is God's love.[136]

God is love that must be converted into loving ...[137].

God is not loving. God is love, the great heart of the universe and of man, from which is drawn forth all feeling, sympathy, emotion, and all that goes to make up the joys of existence.[138]

God is Cause or 1st Cause

A Course in Miracles

Actually, "Cause" is a term properly belonging to God, and His Effect is His Son.[139]

... God is the only Cause.[140]

Unity

God is First Cause, the Principle from which flow all manifestations.[141]

All that man manifests has its origin in a cause that we name Divine Mind.[142]

As there can be but one Cause for all that is, and as that Cause is All-Good, you have a pivotal center from which you can draw conclusions that will settle definitely all the debatable questions of existence.[143]

GOD IS FATHER

A COURSE IN MIRACLES

God Himself keeps your will alive by transmitting it from His Mind to yours as long as there is time. The miracle itself is a reflection of this union of will between Father and Son.[144]

Remember that the Holy Spirit is the communication link between God the Father and His separated Sons.[145]

Your Father created you wholly without sin, wholly without pain, and wholly without suffering of any kind.[146]

For your Father is your Creator, and you are like Him. [147]

UNITY

… God is Father, that man's real source is God, and that his inheritance is the perfection and wholeness of God.[148]

The Father is the every-where-present Spirit in which all that appears has its origin.[149]

METAPHYSICALLY stated, the Father is the God-Mind… [150]

GOD IS PRINCIPLE

"God is Principle" is a fundamental concept in Unity teachings. The term, principle, is found in *A Course in Miracles* and is used more as a modifier than a subject. In Unity, it is often used in a broader context than in *A Course in Miracles*.

A Course in Miracles

The term "principle" in *A Course in Miracles* is used in context different than found in Unity. The intention here is to use principle as a descriptor of a fundamental law or guideline. The first section in Chapter 1 of the Text is entitled "Principles of Miracles." The section then provides 50 principles, or means by which we can identify the miracles that occur in our lives. Additional examples follow. The final quotation is the closest The Course comes to using the term as Unity does, calling the Holy Spirit a "principle."

> The Atonement *principle* was in effect long before the Atonement began. The principle was love and the Atonement was an *act* of love.[151]

> The belief that you must have the impossible in order to be happy is totally at variance with the principle of creation.[152]

> The principle that [is] justice means no one can lose is crucial to this course.[153]

> "The Holy Spirit…is the great correction principle; the bringer of true perception, the inherent power of the vision of Christ.[154]

Unity

In Unity, we find Principle being used in a broader sense as a synonym for God as found in the first two quotes. In the third quote, principle is used much like is found in *A Course in Miracles*.

> The fundamental basis of practical Christianity [Unity] is that God is Principle. Divine Principle is fundamental Truth. God as Principle is the unchangeable life, love, intelligence, and substance of Being.[155]

The truth is, then: That God is Principle, Law, Being, Mind, Spirit, All-Good, omnipotent, omniscient, omnipresent, unchangeable, Creator, Father, Cause, and source of all that is; ... [156]

Father-Principle--The exact and immutable Principle of Being, lying back of all existence as cause, and approachable only along lines of perfect law. It is omnipresent and is not subject to change or open to argument. [157]

The Son of God, The Sonship, Christ

The second part of the Trinity is God's Creation. These terms represent titles given to God's Creation. Throughout Christianity, Jesus has been uniquely given the title of "Son of God" and "Christ." Both Unity and *A Course in Miracles* teach Jesus was not unique. Jesus awakened to Christ Consciousness. Christ Consciousness is our reality too. We are to awaken to Christ as our reality as well.

A Course in Miracles

The Created is the Son. It is the Christ, all of God's creation. In *A Course in Miracles*, the Son, or "Sonship" is recognized completely within God. Further, the Sonship becomes a means by which God continues to create. Furthering Creation is a reason the Son is created. "Sonship" is used to convey the sense of one Son made up of many parts, the coming together of separated consciousness as a single Whole.

> The Son of God is part of the Holy Trinity, but the Trinity Itself is one. ... They are of one Mind and one Will. This single purpose creates perfect integration and establishes the peace of God. [158]

The First Coming of Christ is merely another name for the creation, for Christ is the Son of God.[159]

Without a cause there can be no effects, and yet without effects there is no cause. The cause a cause [is,] is made by its effects; the Father is a Father by His Son. Effects do not create their cause, but they establish its causation. Thus, the son gives Fatherhood to his Creator, and receives the gifts that he has given Him. It is *because* he is God's Son that he must also be a father, who creates as God created him. The circle of creation has no end. [160]

A Course in Miracles also refers to the created Son of God as spirit. Spirit is God's creation.

> *Spirit* is the Thought of God which He created like Himself. The unified spirit is God's one Son, or Christ.[161]

> *Spirit is in a state of grace forever. Your reality* [God's One Son] *is only spirit. Therefore you are in a state of grace forever.*[162]

> …because the mind belongs to spirit which God created and which is therefore eternal.[163]

> [Referring to Gen 1:26] God did create spirit in His Own Thought and of a quality like to His Own. There is nothing else.[164]

> … the Sonship is the sum of all that God created.[165]

> Complete restoration of the Sonship is the only goal of the miracle-minded. [166]

> If all His creations are His Sons, every one must be an integral part of the whole Sonship. The Sonship in its oneness transcends the sum of its parts. However, this is obscured as long as any of

its parts is missing. That is why the conflict cannot ultimately be resolved until all the parts of the Sonship have returned.[167]

UNITY

Unity writings refer to the Son of God, Christ, the Word and the Logos as synonyms. In comparison to *A Course in Miracles* the concept is the same. God, Mind, creates the Son, Christ. And, yet, they are one.

> As the son is to the father, so is the idea to the mind. Mind is one with its ideas, so the Father – God Mind- is one with its offspring, the idea – the Son.[168]

> In every person the Christ, or the Word of God, is infolded; it is an idea that contains ideas.[169]

> Logos – The Word of God; the divine archetype idea that contains all ideas: the Christ, the Son of God, spiritual man in manifestation.[170]

> "Christ" is not a person. It is not Jesus.[171]

> Son of God--The fullness of the perfect-man idea in Divine Mind, the Christ. ... The living Word; the Christ idea in the Mind of God.
> The Son ever exists in God. Father and Son are one and are omnipresent in man and the universe. ... Christ is that idea in the Absolute (Son of God).[172]

THE HOLY SPIRIT

The Holy Spirit is not the third person in the Trinity or a dove as depicted in the story of Jesus' baptism. It is not something separate that guides and directs us. The Holy Spirit is that part of Mind that is still awake in our seeming separated mind that we can utilize to make the highest and best choices in our lives. In our experience, the Holy Spirit seems to be a lot of things, not because It *is* a lot of things. The Holy Spirit seems this way because we are making up the experience that best fulfills our current needs based on our sense consciousness.

A Course in Miracles

> The Holy Spirit is the only part of the Holy Trinity that has a symbolic function. He is referred to as the Healer, the Comforter and the Guide.[173]

> The Holy Spirit is described as the remaining Communication Link between God and His separated Sons. In order to fulfill this special function the Holy Spirit has assumed a dual function. He knows because He is part of God: He perceives because He was sent to save humanity. ... [174]

As a gentle reminder, the male-centric language used in these quotes can distract from understanding what is being communicated. In this paragraph, the language implies the Holy Spirit is genderless since it is in our mind. Note, also, if the "Holy Spirit abides in the part of mind that is part of Christ Mind" this means that the Holy Spirit is Mind as well.

> The Holy Spirit abides in the part of your mind that is part of the Christ Mind. He represents your Self and your Creator, Who are one. He speaks for God and also for you, being joined with both. And therefore it is He Who proves them one. He seems to be a Voice, for in that form He speaks God's Word to you. He seems to be a Guide through a far country, for you need that form of help. He seems to be whatever meets the needs you think you have. But He is not deceived when you perceive yourself entrapped in needs

you do not have [in spite of your belief in them]. It is from these He would deliver you. It is from [your belief in] these that He would make you safe.[175]

He [The Holy Spirit] is part of the Holy Trinity because His Mind is partly yours and also partly God's.[176]

Yet He [God] has created the Holy Spirit as the Mediator between perception and knowledge. Without this link with God, perception would have replaced knowledge forever in your mind. With this link with God, perception will become so changed and purified that it will lead to knowledge. That is its function as the Holy Spirit sees it. Therefore that is its function in truth. [177]

"Jesus is the manifestation of the Holy Spirit."[178]

"You are His [the Holy Spirit's] manifestation in this world."[179]

Now hear God speak to you, through Him [Holy Spirit] Who is His Voice and yours as well…[180]

God's Voice will answer, for He [Holy Spirit] speaks for you and for your Father. [181]

UNITY

The Holy Spirit is our awareness of the activity of God or Divine Mind at the point of our consciousness. Like *A Course in Miracles*, the Holy Spirit is described as a connecting link. In addition, many quotes from Unity writings would lead one to the interpretation that the Holy Spirit is somehow male and separate. Myrtle Fillmore gives us a wonderful view of the Holy Spirit that resonates with the view presented in *A Course in Miracles*.

The Holy Spirit is the activity of God-mind in the consciousness of man. The long way, the most difficult way, back to the Father's house is the way of experience; the short cut is being receptive and obedient to the leading of the Holy Spirit in thought, word and deed, putting God first in your life.[182]

We all need a better acquaintance with that phase of creative Mind that reveals and forms a connecting link between the Most High and the mind of the natural man. Most of us have not made conscious contact with the Spirit within but are thinking and acting in the outer crust of our being.[183]

The Holy Spirit is the action or outpouring or activity of the living Word. This activity produces what may be termed the light of Spirit, the breath of God, the "personality" of Being.[184]

The Holy Spirit is…the whole Spirit of God in action. It is God's word in movement: the working, moving, breathing, brooding Spirit. …The Holy Spirit is the law of God in action; in that action God appears as having individuality. It is the personality of Being. It is neither the all of Being nor the fullness of Christ, but is an emanation, or breath, sent -forth to do a definite work.[185]

Summary

Clearly, both *A Course in Miracles* and Unity refer to the Holy Trinity. Each in its own way dispatches the traditional definitions of the Trinity. Each "person" of the traditional Trinity is redefined into aspects of God-Mind. God is not a person, entity or being. God is NOT a Being or the Being. God is Being (Beingness).

CHAPTER 4

Who is Jesus, Who am I?

INTRODUCTION

TRADITIONAL CHRISTIANITY STIPULATES JESUS IS the one and only Son of God. God sent him here to save humanity from their sins. Jesus is the "only begotten Son," the Christ. Each person is innately a sinner and not the son of God. In this sense, humankind would appear to be more like stepchildren.

Both Unity and *A Course in Miracles* present Jesus differently. Words attributed to Jesus in the Bible have been misconstrued; traditional Christianity is about Jesus saving us from our sins. Unity and *A Course in Miracles* represent Jesus as one of us who awakened to the Christ reality, which is ours too. In this sense, Jesus is our teacher, example, and way-shower. The intention of both teachings is to provide a means to realize Christ Nature through viewing ourselves, life, and the world differently.

JESUS, THE MAN

Both teachings agree that Jesus was a person just like us.

A COURSE IN MIRACLES

The name of Jesus is the name of one who was a man but saw the face of Christ in all his brothers, and remembered God. So he became identified with *Christ*, a man no longer, but at one with God. ... In his complete identification with the Christ—the perfect Son of God, His one creation and His happiness, forever like Himself and one with Him—Jesus became what all of you must be. He led the way for you to follow him.[186]

Throughout *A Course in Miracles*, there is a frequent use of "I." Twelve of these are references from the Bible, speaking of "I" as God, I as the Holy Spirit, or "I" as the Christ. All others (2,552) correspond to Jesus the Christ as the source of the material that Helen Schucman scribed. Amidst all of these citations there are only a few that refer to Jesus as a man, or a separated son.

I [Jesus] could not understand their [the ego and the body] importance to you if I had not once been tempted to believe in them myself.[187]

Unity

He (Jesus) was man on the quest, man making the great discovery of His divinity, man breaking through the psychological barrier between humankind and God, man proving the Christ in humankind and his or her inherent potential for overcoming, for eternal life.[188]

The Man of Nazareth ... Jesus was keenly conscious of the character of God and his own relationship to God. He knew God as unlimited love and as ever-present, abundant life; he knew God as wisdom and supply. He knew God as Father, who is ever ready and willing to supply every need of the human heart.[189]

We cannot separate Jesus Christ from God or tell where man leaves off and God begins in Him. To say that we are men as Jesus

Christ was a man is not exactly true, because He had dropped that personal consciousness by which we separate ourselves from our true God self. He became consciously one with the absolute principle of Being. He proved in His resurrection and ascension that He had no consciousness separate from that of Being, therefore He really was this Being to all intents and purposes. Yet He attained no more than what is expected of every one of us....[190]

Who am I?

This is a question both teachings address. Our focus has been on our Reality, as God's Creation. Here, we focus on the individuals we "think" we are; who we define ourselves to be when we think of ourselves as bodies, individual minds, or personalities. As seemingly separated individuals, we believe life is limited to our physical existence.

Although we believe we are separated individuals, this is not our reality. Both teachings refer to the same scripture (Genesis 2:21) to address what seemed to occur:

A Course in Miracles

Yet the Bible says a deep sleep fell upon Adam, and nowhere is there reference to his waking up. The world has not yet experienced a comprehensive reawakening or rebirth. Such a rebirth is impossible as long as you continue to project or miscreate.[191]

Unity

A limited concept of Jehovah God caused a deep sleep (mesmeric state) to fall on the man (Adam). Nowhere in Scripture is there any record to show that Adam was ever fully awakened; and he (man) is still partly in this dreamlike state of consciousness. In this state he creates a world of his own and peoples it with ideas corresponding to his own sleep-benumbed consciousness.[192]

Our Current Perceived State

The ideas and beliefs we develop and use to live our life are not always based on the Knowledge of God. Both teachings maintain that our conscious state is a derivation of our separated state of mind; it is a state of perception. Ideas and beliefs we develop in our separated mind, are subsequently accepted as "real," and are projected outwards making the world we see.

A Course in Miracles

In *A Course in Miracles*, the definition of the ego is what we think of as our "true self" in a separated state of consciousness. From the *Glossary-Index for A Course in Miracles*, we find a definition of the ego, which could be said to describe what we think is our true self when in a separated state of consciousness:

> Ego- the belief in the reality of the separated or false self, made as substitute for the Self which God created; the thought of separation that gives rise to sin, guilt, fear, and a thought system based on specialness to protect itself; that part of the mind that believes it is separate from the Mind of Christ;...
>
> (Note—not to be equated with the "ego" of psychoanalysis, but can be equated with the entire psyche, of which the psychoanalytic "ego" is a part.)[193]

> Everyone makes an ego or a self for himself, which is subject to enormous variation because of its instability. ...

> Your own state of mind is a good example of how the ego was made. When you threw Knowledge [the Knowledge of God] away it is as if you never had it. …
>
> No one dismisses something he considers part of himself. You react to your ego much as God does to His creations, --with love, protection and charity.[194]

If you cannot hear the Voice for God, it is because you do not choose to listen. That you do listen to the voice of your ego is demonstrated by your attitudes, your feelings and your behavior. Yet this is what you want. This is what you are fighting to keep and what you are vigilant to save. Your mind is filled with schemes to save the face of your ego, and you do not seek the face of Christ. The glass in which the ego seeks to see its face is dark indeed. How can it maintain the trick of its existence except with mirrors? But where you look to find yourself is up to you.[195]

…the ego is not you.[196]

We also identify ourselves as our body, which is an extension of the thought system of the ego:

> The body is the ego's home by its own election. It is the only identification with which the ego feels safe, since the body's vulnerability is its own best argument that you cannot be of God. This is a belief the ego sponsors eagerly.[197]

> Everything you recognize you identify with externals, something outside itself. You cannot even think of God without a body, or in some form you think you recognize. …
>
> The body is a tiny fence around a little part of a glorious and complete idea. It draws a circle, infinitely small, around a very little segment of Heaven, splintered from the whole, proclaiming that within it is your kingdom where God can enter not.[198]

Freedom must be impossible as long as you perceive a body as yourself. The body is a limit. Who would seek for freedom in a body looks for it where it cannot be found. The mind can be made free when it no longer sees itself as in a body, firmly tied to it and sheltered by its presence.[199]

Unity

What The Course terms "ego," Fillmore refers to as "personality," the "ego," or "the adverse ego." The personality is who we think we are; a personality manifesting and inhabiting a body.

> ego, adverse--When the ego attaches itself to sense consciousness, it builds the antichrist man, who has no basis in reality. This is known as the adverse ego. It is the adverse ego that causes all the trouble in the world. Its selfishness and greed make men grovel in the mire of materiality, when they might soar in the heavens of spirituality.[200]

> ego--The I. The ego is man, and by reason of his divinity he makes and remakes as he wills. In this lie his greatest strength and his greatest weakness. The ego of itself is possessed of nothing. It is a mere ignorant child of innocence floating in the Mind of Being, but through the door of its consciousness must pass all the treasures of God.[201]

> [Personality is] The sum total of characteristics that each person has personalized as distinct of himself or herself, independent of others or of divine principle. ... Personality is what people seem to be when they think in their three-dimensional consciousness.[202]

> Personality applies to the human part of you—the person, the external. ... When you say that you dislike anyone, you mean that

you dislike his or her personality—that exterior something that presents itself from the outside. It is the outer, changeable man, in contradistinction to the inner or real man.[203]

As in *A Course in Miracles,* Unity agrees that man is not the body.

Now, mark you, man is not solely his body, for man is more than body, but without a body there could be no visible man. ... You see at once that man is not body, but that the body is the declaration of man, the substantial expression of his mind. We see so many different types of men that we are bound to admit that the body is merely the individual's specific interpretation of himself, whatever it may be. Man is an unknown quantity; we see merely the various ideas of man expressed in terms of body, but not man himself. The identification of man is determined by the individual himself, and he expresses his conception of man in his body.[204]

Christ, Son of God, the Sonship

These are all terms used to refer to "God's one creation." Just as God is not a person, being or entity, Christ is not a person being or entity, even though the language of both teachings would certainly make it seem that way. In Platonic terms, Christ is the idea or ideal of personhood; Christ is the absolute principle of being. Christ encompasses all created beings and all creation. As the Bible says, "Christ is all and in all" (Col. 3:11).

A Course in Miracles

God's "One Creation" is referred to throughout the material as "the Son" and "the Sonship:"

It should especially be noted that God has only one Son. If all his creations are His Sons, every one must be an integral part of the whole Sonship. The Sonship in its oneness transcends the sum of its parts.[205]

God created His Sons by extending His Thought, and retaining the extensions of His Thought in His Mind. All His Thoughts are thus perfectly united within themselves and with each other. ... God created you to create. You cannot extend His Kingdom until you know of its wholeness.[206]

I have assured you that the Mind that decided for me [Jesus] is also in you, and that you can let it change you just as it changed me.[207]

Nothing can prevail against a Son of God who commends his spirit into the Hands of his Father. By doing this the mind awakens from its sleep and remembers its Creator.[208]

Unity

Christ" is not a person. It is not Jesus. Christ is a degree of stature that Jesus attained, but a degree of potential stature that dwells in every man.[209]

The man that God created in His own image and likeness and pronounced good and very good is spiritual man. This man is the direct offspring of Divine Mind, God's idea of perfect man. This is the only begotten Son, the Christ, the Lord God, the Jehovah, the I AM.[210]

The Christ man or true man is the perfect ideal, and humanity is that ideal on the way of realization.[211]

Christ abides in each person as ... potential perfection. ... Each person has within himself or herself the Christ Idea, just as Jesus had. Each person must look to the indwelling Christ in order to recognize ... their divine origin and birth.[212]

In every person the Christ, or Word of God, is enfolded; it is an idea that contains ideas.[213]

The creature that you have seemed to be will no longer appear. The new man, image and likeness of God [Christ], will become manifest when you awaken to the consciousness of it.[214]

Summary

An Overview of Our One Mission

Here are some quotations that address what Jesus attained, and what is humanity's ultimate purpose. You will note *A Course in Miracles* refers to a "universal experience," and emphasizes one theology is impossible for all of humanity.

A Course in Miracles

...a universal theology is impossible, but a universal experience is not only possible but necessary" (Manual, p. 77) Although Christian in statement, The Course deals with universal spiritual themes. It emphasizes that it is but one version of the universal curriculum. There are many others, this one differing from them only in form. They all lead to God in the end.[215]

There is nothing about me [Jesus] you cannot attain. I have nothing that does not come from God. The difference between us now is that I have nothing else. This leaves me in a state which is only potential in you.[216]

Unity

Christ abides in each person as ... potential perfection. ... Each person has within himself or herself the Christ Idea, just as Jesus had. Each person must look to the indwelling Christ in order to recognize ... their divine origin and birth.[217]

The more you think about the Christ within, the stronger will grow your consciousness of the divine presence and your oneness with Him, until you can "be still, and know that I am God.[218]

The one and only object of humankind's existence is the development of his or her soul, and any attainment, whether mental or material, that cannot be associated with and counted as an aid toward that end will ultimately be refused.[219]

CHAPTER 5

Separation, Relative Mind and the Ego

SEPARATION

ALTHOUGH *A COURSE IN MIRACLES* and Unity both teach there is only Oneness, the idea of separation must be addressed. It is the intention of both teachings to reveal the nature of separation beliefs in our lives. Both teach that the idea and belief in separation gives rise to the experience of separation in consciousness, and subsequently to the physical universe. (Refer to our discussion on the Concepts of the World and the Universe- Chapter 10)

A COURSE IN MIRACLES

Here is what *A Course in Miracles* says about the separation.

> There is no separation of God and His creation[220]. ...the separation is no more than an illusion of despair[221]. ...The full awareness of the Atonement, then, is the recognition that *the separation never occurred.*[222]

> Into eternity, where all is one, there crept a tiny, mad idea, [the idea of separation] at which the Son of God remembered not to laugh. In his forgetting did the thought become a serious idea, and possible of both accomplishment and real effects.[223]

Let us look closer at the whole illusion that what you made has power to enslave its maker. This is the same belief that caused the separation. It is the meaningless idea that thoughts can leave the thinker's mind, be different from it and in opposition to it.[224]

The world you perceive is a world of separation....The world you made is therefore totally chaotic, governed by arbitrary and senseless "laws," and without meaning of any kind.[225]

What you believe is true for you. In this sense the separation *has* occurred, and to deny it is merely to use denial inappropriately. However, to concentrate on error is only a further error.[226]

UNITY

The following quotes on the experience of separation and the solution speak for themselves.

This Mind exists as the absolute, the unlimited. In its consciousness there is no apartness, no separation, and whoever puts himself into its consciousness can accomplish things instantly.[227]

There is no absence or separation in God. His omnipresence is your omnipresence. There can be no absence in Mind. If God were for one instant separated from His creations, they would immediately fall into dissolution. In spirit and in truth you can never for one instant be separated from the life activity of God.[228]

This is the first step in the fall of man--the belief that he can act wisely without first knowing the plan of God.

This fall takes place in his own consciousness. He follows the dictates of the animal nature rather than those of the higher wisdom, ...which is a consciousness of nakedness and separation from God.[229]

The conscious I can look in two directions--to the outer world where the thoughts that rise within it give sensation and feeling, which ultimate in a moving panorama of visibility; or to the world within, whence all its life, power, and intelligence are derived. When the I looks wholly within, it loses all sense of the external.... When it looks wholly without, upon sensation and feeling, it loses its bearings in the maze of its own thought creations. Then it builds up a belief of separateness from, and independence of, a causing power. Man sees only form and makes his God a personal being located in a city of dimensions. This belief of separateness leads to ignorance, because all intelligence is derived from the one Divine Mind, and when the soul thinks itself something alone, it cuts itself off in consciousness from the fount of inspiration. Believing himself separate from his source, man loses sight of the divine harmony.[230]

In its spiritual character our mind blends with Divine Mind as the mist blends with the cloud. Both are composed of the same elements and they unite without friction if left to their natural affinity. But give "the mist" the power and ability of [belief in] separation and we have conditions that involve divisions beyond enumeration. Man came out of God, is of the same mind elements, and exists within the mind of God always. Yet by thinking that he is separate from omnipresent Spirit he has set up a mental state of apartness from his source and he dwells in ignorance of that which is nearer to him than hands and feet.[231]

Relative Mind

For clarity, we use the term "relative mind" to define that state of our mind that believes we exist separate from God. Both teachings emphasize the importance of our understanding the "relative mind." The relative mind consists of the conscious and subconscious minds. It is the mind we use to be aware of what is going on in our day-to-day lives.

Much of what we experience in our relative mind is based on information gleaned from the input of our five senses. This includes the beliefs we get from the culture in which we are raised, as well as those in collective consciousness (not the Divine Mind). All manner of discontent, separation, fear and anger are rooted here. We might even say the purpose of these teachings is to awaken us to the distinction between our relative mind and God-Mind (Christ-Mind).

Both teachings clearly state there is One Mind - the Mind of God. Usually Mind/God-Mind is distinguished from relative mind/mind by capitalizing references to God-Mind. Other times the distinction is discerned by context. The relative mind focuses on a separation based consciousness. That mind is what we think of as our individuated selves; the ego-based thought system which perpetuates the relative mind. Ironically, it is also the starting point of awakening to our Oneness. Regardless of our belief, the relative mind can never be separated from God-Mind.

A Course in Miracles

Two definitions from the *Glossary-Index for A Course in Miracles* can be used to address the separated mind; mind and the Mind of God.

> mind, perception- the agent of choice; we are free to believe that our minds can be separated or split off from the Mind of God (wrong-mindedness), or that they can be returned to it (right-mindedness);[232]

Mind of God- equated with the creative function of God which represents the activating agent of spirit, supplying its creative energy; as an extension of God, the Mind of Christ…after the separation, the Mind of Christ *appeared* to be split in two: Mind and mind.[233]

The "split mind" is the focus of our discussion here.

Your mind is dividing its allegiance between two kingdoms, and you are totally committed to neither. Your identification with the Kingdom is totally beyond question except by you, when you are thinking insanely. What you are is not established by your perception, and is not influenced by it at all.[234]

Consciousness, the level of perception, was the first split introduced into the mind after the separation, making the mind a perceiver rather than a creator. Consciousness is correctly identified as the domain of the ego. The ego is the wrong-minded attempt to perceive yourself as you wish to be, rather than as you are….

The ego is the questioning aspect of the post-separation self, which was made rather than created. It is capable of asking questions, but not perceiving meaningful answers, because these would involve knowledge and cannot be perceived. The mind is therefore confused, because only One-mindedness can be without confusion. A separated or divided mind *must* be confused. It is necessarily uncertain about what it is. It has to be in conflict because it is out of accord with itself.[235]

Perception always involves some misuse of mind, because it brings the mind into areas of uncertainty. The mind is very active. When it chooses to be separated it chooses to perceive. Until then, it wills only to know. Afterwards it can only choose ambiguously, and the only way out of ambiguity is clear perception. The mind returns to its proper function only when it wills to know. This places it in the service of spirit, where perception is changed. The mind chooses to divide itself when it chooses to make its own levels. But it could not entirely separate itself from spirit, because it is from spirit that it derives its whole power to make or create.[236]

A Course in Miracles teaches about the states of right and wrong mindedness. Wrong-mindedness represents the thinking that perpetuates the separated thought system. No pursuit of a higher consciousness occurs here; instead, the thinking focuses on individual survival as alone and separate. Right-mindedness represents the aspect of the mind that, while believing it is separate, directs its thinking towards correcting this mistaken belief.

> *Right-mindedness* listens to the Holy Spirit, forgives the world, and through Christ's vision sees the real world in its place. ...
> *Wrong-mindedness* listens to the ego and makes illusions; perceiving sin and justifying anger, and seeing guilt, disease and death as real. Both this world and the real world are illusions because right-mindedness merely overlooks, or forgives what never happened.[237]

> Right mindedness is not to be confused with the knowing mind [Christ-Mind or God-Mind], because it is applicable only to right perception [perception directed towards healing the belief in separation]. ...The term "right-mindedness" is properly used as the correction for "wrong-mindedness" [separation-based consciousness], and applies to the state of mind that induces accurate perception.[238]

> The ego is a wrong-minded attempt to perceive yourself as you wish to be, rather than as you are.[239]

> Salvation is nothing more than "right-mindedness," which is not the One-mindedness of the Holy Spirit, but which must be achieved

before One-mindedness is restored. Right-mindedness leads to the next step automatically, because right perception is uniformly without attack, and therefore wrong-mindedness is obliterated.[240]

UNITY

Unity explains and defines the relative mind in many ways. It is clear that there are aspects of this mind that leads us away from the awareness of Oneness into the morass of separation. And yet, it is through the pivotal nature of this mind that we begin to awaken to Oneness and end separation.

> mind--The starting point of every act and thought and feeling; the common meeting ground of God and man. God is mind, and we cannot describe God with human language, so we cannot describe mind. We can only say: I am mind; I know. God is mind; He knows.[241]

> mind, carnal--Misuse of mind powers, arising from ignorance of the relationship between God and man. A state of consciousness formed about a false ego or false concept of man. All the "works of the flesh" are the product of carnal mind (derived from Galatians 5:19).[242]

> mind, mortal – Error consciousness in unregenerate man, or man composed of ungodlike thoughts. It is the opposite of the Christ Mind, which is the perfect Mind of God in man. Mortal mind gathers its information through the senses. It judges by appearances, which are often false judgments. Man must renounce this false state of mind if he is to be one with God. Mortal mind breeds sin, poverty, sickness, and death.[243]

The mind is the seat of perception of the things we see, hear, and feel. It is through the mind that we see the beauties of the earth and sky, of music, of art, in fact, of everything. That silent shuttle of thought working in and out through cell and nerve weaves into one harmonious whole the myriad moods of mind, and we call it life.[244]

mind, change of--A change of mind is the very first requisite of the new life in Christ. We go into this new and higher state of consciousness as we would go into another country. The kingdom of heaven is right here in our midst and will become tangible reality to us when we have developed the faculties necessary to comprehend it.[245]

Even though the relative mind is the source of our belief in separation, it is never separate from Divine Mind/Mind.

The one Mind is a unit and cannot be divided. The individual mind is a state of consciousness in the one Mind.[246]

one Mind--There is but one Mind. Every individual and the various phases of character that make that individual are but states of consciousness in the one Mind.[247]

The Ego

In Unity and *A Course in Miracles*, both theologies present an essential message: the reason for the existence of these teachings. Both recognize humankind has strayed from home; our life is lived from a state that believes we are separate from God. The only place this seems to exist is within our beliefs, and these beliefs are maintained by the ego thought system. It is our relinquishment of this belief of separation that enables us to know we are created in the image and likeness of God. (Derived from Gen. 1:26)

The ego thought system is pervasive. In the absence of any guidance or correction, our perceptions, our way of seeing the world, our way of seeing ourselves, and our way of dealing with anyone else occur through the ego-based thought system. Herein lies the source of fear, pain, sickness, loneliness, doubt, anger, and even our belief in death.

The difference between the two teachings lies in matters of semantics. Their commonality speaks to the resolution: All perceptions that flow from the ego based thought system are forgiven or released and replaced with perceptions that are based on our higher consciousness. Both teachings describe this process in a manner that is moving towards the same end result. What differs is the description of the realm of the ego and what it conveys.

Within *A Course in Miracles*, the ego is identified as an error thought system. It is always wrong, as it furthers the belief in separation. It is an illusion. *A Course in Miracles* does speak of moving our consciousness to "true perception" a state where every ego based thought is forgiven immediately and replaced with a perception derived from a consciousness of love. Unity recognizes the pervasive presence of the ego thought system, and speaks for its transition from a "sense based ego" to a "spiritual ego," to the attainment of the Christ mind Jesus realized. Whether labeled as "true perception" or the "spiritual ego," both teachings are leading towards relinquishment of the separation-based thought system that humankind has come to rely on in our day to day living.

A Course in Miracles

The *Glossary-Index for A Course in Miracles Keyed to the second edition*, written by Kenneth Wapnick, Ph.D, begins with an introduction to the theory behind *A Course in Miracles*:

> *A Course in Miracles*, therefore, is written on two levels, reflecting two basic divisions. The first level presents the difference between the One Mind and the separated mind, while the second contrasts wrong-and right-mindedness within the separated mind. On this first level, for example, the world and body are illusions made by the ego, and thus symbolizes separation. The second level relates

to this world where we believe we are. Here, the world and the body are neutral and serve one of two purposes. To the wrong-minded ego they are instruments to reinforce separation; to the right mind they are the Holy Spirit's teaching devices through which we learn His lessons of forgiveness.[248]

Throughout *A Course in Miracles* we find references to our mind being split. At the highest level, this split represents the distinction between the Absolute Mind (where we are "One with God"--no separation, non-duality), and our separated mind (the individuated mind, the ego mind) believing we are apart from God. The separated mind is an illusion, it is a dream. Our belief in this separation is found in our lives daily--the world we perceive is perpetuated through this thought system.

> The ego is nothing more than a part of your belief about yourself.[249]

> The ego is the part of the mind that believes your existence is defined by separation.[250]

> The ego is idolatry; the sign of limited and separated self, born in a body, doomed to suffer and to end its life in death.[251]

> Consciousness is correctly identified as the domain of the ego. The ego is a wrong-minded attempt to perceive yourself as you wish to be, rather than as you are.[252]

> ...the ego is not you.[253]

The *Glossary-Index for A Course in Miracles*, provides a definition of the ego useful in this discussion. We'll address this in two components, first the definition of the ego.

> ego-- The belief in the reality of the separated or false self, made as substitute for the Self which God created; the thought

of separation that gives rise to sin, guilt and fear, and a thought system based on attack to protect itself; the part of the mind that believes it is separate from the Mind of Christ...

"NOTE—not to be equated with the "ego" of psychoanalysis, but can be roughly equated with the entire psyche, of which the psychoanalytic "ego" is a part.[254]

Next, at the level of this dream or illusion (the world as we believe it to be), there seems to be another split of the separated mind into what is termed the wrong mindedness and right mindedness. Wrong-mindedness is when we see and live life only from the ego thought system. We can seem to be lost in it. Yet, however firmly we believe in "wrong mindedness," there is a part of the split mind, "right-mindedness" that knows there is something different; there must be a better way. It knows all we see in the wrong-minded state cannot be real, or the Truth. Right-mindedness is that state of the mind which questions all decisions and judgments made through the ego. It is right-mindedness which looks to a higher resolution, looks for the loving answer to all matters, rather than to perpetuate fear. Continuing from the above *Glossary-Index* quote:

> ...this split mind has two parts: wrong- and right-mindedness; ego is almost always used to denote 'wrong-mindedness," but can include "right-mindedness," the part of the ego that can learn....[255]

> Wrong-mindedness: the part of our separated and split minds that contains the ego—the voice of sin, guilt, fear and attack....[256]

> Right-mindedness—the part of our separated minds that contains the Holy Spirit—the Voice of forgiveness and reason...[257]

From the text of *A Course in Miracles* we learn:

> The term "right-mindedness" is properly used as the correction for "wrong-mindedness" and applies to the state of mind that

induces accurate perception. It is miracle-minded in view of how you perceive yourself.[258]

The following statement from the *Workbook for Students* describes the distinction of the mind as used by Spirit, and the split mind derived from our wrong-minded thinking.

> Spirit makes use of mind as means to find its Self-expression. And the mind which serves the spirit is at peace and filled with joy. Its power comes from spirit, and it is fulfilling happily its function here. Yet mind can also see itself divorced from spirit, and perceive itself within a body it confuses with itself. Without its function then it has no peace, and happiness is alien to its thoughts.[259]

Judgment is another example of wrong-mindedness:

> You have often been urged to refrain from judging, not because it is a right to be withheld from you. You cannot judge. You merely can believe the ego's judgments, all of which are false. It guides your senses carefully, to prove how weak you are; how helpless and afraid, how apprehensive of just punishment, how black, with sin, how wretched in your guilt.[260]

We should also consider how we think of the ego, and our life as perceived from the ego:

> No one dismisses something he considers part of himself. You react to your ego much as God does to His creation,--with love protection and charity. ...The question is not how you respond to the ego, but what you believe you are. Belief is an ego function, and as long as your origin is open to belief you are regarding it from an ego viewpoint. ...Belief that there is another way of perceiving is the loftiest idea of which ego thinking is capable. That is because it contains a hint of recognition that the ego is not the Self. ...

The ego regards the body as its home, and tries to satisfy itself through the body. But the idea that this is possible is a decision of the mind, which has become completely confused about what is really possible.[261]

The ego is a confusion in identification. Never having had a consistent model, it never developed consistently. It is the product of the misapplication of the laws of God by distorted minds that are misusing their power. ...

Do not be afraid of the ego. It depends on your mind and as you made it by believing in it, so you can dispel it by withdrawing belief from it. ...

The Holy Spirit will teach you to perceive beyond your belief, because the truth is beyond belief and His perception is true. ...

The whole purpose of this course is to teach you that the ego is unbelievable and will forever be unbelievable. You who made the ego by believing the unbelievable cannot make this judgment alone. By accepting the Atonement for yourself, you are deciding against the belief that you can be alone, thus dispelling the idea of separation and affirming your true identification with the whole Kingdom as literally part of you. This identification is as beyond doubt as it is beyond belief. Your wholeness has no limits because being is infinity.[262]

UNITY

From *The Revealing Word*, we find the following definition for the ego:

ego—the I. The ego is man, and by reason of his divinity he makes and remakes as he wills. In this lie his greatest strength and his greatest weakness. The ego of itself is possessed of nothing. It is a mere ignorant child of innocence floating in the Mind of Being, but through the door of its consciousness must pass all the treasures of God.[263]

Sense consciousness and Race consciousness are terms used to describe the ego or personality. The former represents thoughts based on physical sensations; the later represents thoughts based on cultural beliefs, passed on through history or based on current cultural decisions. Either way, they represent the consciousness of ego, derived through the "ignorant child" referred to above. The relinquishment of these beliefs leads to the discovery of the spiritual ego, the direction towards the divine.

> ego, spiritual--The true self; an individualized center of God consciousness; I AM; conscious identity.[264]

In *Mysteries of Genesis*, Charles Fillmore provides a metaphysical description of Abram and the King of Sodom that speaks to the spiritual ego and the personal ego, respectively:

> Abram represents the spiritual ego, and the King of Sodom represents the personal, the physical ego. The spiritual ego or spiritual man has its first development on the physical plane. The two egos, the spiritual and the physical, are united there in appropriating physical things, personal things, that they consider valuable, such as appetites, passions, and other things on the sense plane. The spiritual man advances or develops beyond that. He does not want these things, so he gives them all to the personality, the physical ego. Then the physical man is willing to give up anything to the spiritual man, and he will claim that he supplied the spiritual man. That is the glorification of the personality. The personal man claims that he is the whole thing, that everything belongs to him. It is personal selfishness, and the spiritual man does not want to be told that he got anything from the physical. He gets his things from the realm of ideas, the spiritual realm.

Man is prone to feel that the outer or sense world is the source of his good, at least a measure of it. But in order fully to realize our Sonship and our divine heritage, we must hold fast to Spirit. We must see Spirit as our only cause and sustenance. We have a tendency to plead the cause of the good in our sense nature. This is characteristic of all of us. We try hard to save some of our sense thoughts and secret habits. We have indulged in them so long (and our ancestors before us did likewise, beyond the memory of man) that we cannot help thinking there is some good in them. However we, like Abraham, must keep our vision high. We must hold steadfastly to the realization that God is the one source of all, that in spirit and in truth.[265]

Charles Fillmore, in *Christian Healing*, also provides a description associated with the Apostle Paul:

I die daily," said Paul. The "I" that dies daily is personal consciousness, formed of fear, ignorance, disease, the lust for material possessions, pride, anger, and the legion of demons that cluster about the personal ego. The only Savior of this one is Christ, the spiritual ego, the superconsciousness. We cannot, in our own strength, solve the great, self-purifying problem, but by giving ourselves wholly to Christ and constantly denying the demands of the personal self, we grow into the divine image. This is the process by which we "awake, with *beholding* thy form.[266]

Summary

Using somewhat different terminology, both Unity and *A Course in Miracles* picture us as responding to one of two opposing voices: 1. the ego or the Holy Spirit in The Course's terminology. 2. Sense consciousness (personal ego), or Christ consciousness (spiritual ego), Holy Spirit, in

Unity's terminology. Our task, in its simplest terms, is the choice between these two voices. Which voice are we listening to? Is it a voice based on fear, or one based on love? Is it a voice urging separation in some sense, or a voice encouraging union and the recognition of Oneness?

CHAPTER 6

Specialness

—⚋—

Author's note:
We begin this chapter with a definition of specialness to establish a starting point for what will follow.
According to the Merriam-Webster On-Line Dictionary, "specialness" is not a word. The dictionary does define "ness" as "a state or condition," and "special" as "distinguished by some unusual quality ... . For the purposes of our discussion, "specialness" is "a state or condition that is distinguished by some unusual quality."
We believe that this chapter will provide a most evident example of the distinction between our everyday means of thinking and our universal reality.

Introduction

The concept of specialness is strongly emphasized in *A Course in Miracles*. Initially, it is addressed in the context of our True Reality; we are all "equally special," (a concept we will examine in more detail in a moment). Later, a large amount of the material is about specialness in the context of our perception-based state and how to resolve it. *A Course in Miracles* recognizes the importance of relationships in our awakening, it's not difficult to recognize the extent to which specialness applies within our relationships.

Our considering specialness and special relationships becomes a means of addressing the nature of our ego-based living. It is the unholy instant (defined below) that begins the spiral into specialness; it is the Holy Instant where we align ourselves with the Holy Spirit and correct errant thoughts of unique specialness. Wrong mindedness becomes right mindedness. Specialness translates into holiness; special relationships translate into holy relationships.

Unity does not address this concept of specialness directly because the primary focus is on the ways and means of realizing Christ Consciousness and Oneness; *A Course in Miracles*' primary focus is on undoing the ego-based belief system in order to realize our Christ Consciousness and Oneness, and its central means for doing so is our relationships. However, while not referring directly to "specialness" there are some commonalities. When appropriate we will add supporting quotes from Unity writings.

ALL MY BROTHERS ARE SPECIAL

A COURSE IN MIRACLES

Early in *A Course in Miracles*, emphasis is placed on our Oneness with God. A couple of statements speak of our "specialness" in Universal Oneness, fully of God.

> The specialness of God's Sons does not stem from exclusion but from inclusion. All my brothers are special. If they are deprived of anything, their perception becomes distorted. When this occurs the whole family of God, or the Sonship, is impaired in its relationships.[267]

> God loves every brother as He Loves you; neither less nor more. He needs them all equally, and so do you.[268]

Inclusion speaks to our Oneness with God and one another. God knows us and loves us as one, the Son of God. There is no exclusion in the oneness of God-Love.

The rest of this chapter is provided to show how special exclusion plays out in our daily lives. All specialness has fear and hate as its foundation. In specialness, people are excluded and not accepted because they do not have what we want. This is special hate. People are accepted and loved because they have what we think we want. This is special love. Notice that special love is based on the exclusion of others.

Unity

Unity shares similar views about our "universal specialness" and equality.

> The cry goes up: "This is foolish, sacrilegious, to put man beside Jesus Christ and claim that they are equals." The claim is not that humans, in their present consciousness, are equal with Jesus, but that they must be equal with Him before they will emerge from the sense of delusion in which they now wander.[269]

> Jesus recognized divine sonship and universal brotherhood. We confess Jesus as the Son of God, and by that confession we acknowledge that all men are sons of God.[270]

> The grace of God extends to all people, not alone to one sect or creed. All men are equal in favor with God.[271]

> We do not abandon our friends and withdraw all interest in them, but we recognize their equality with ourselves in the supreme Mind, and by that recognition they are freed from a mental dependency with which we have unconsciously bound them. They begin to assert their inherent capacities; they step forth with the work that Spirit within them has chosen.[272]

Dreams of Specialness

A Course in Miracles

> The special ones are all asleep, surrounded by a world of loveliness they do not see. Freedom and peace and joy stand there, beside the bier on which they sleep, and call them to come forth and awaken from their dream of death. Yet they hear nothing. They are lost in dreams of specialness. They hate the call that would awaken them, and they curse God because He did not make their dream [of being specially loved by God] reality.[273]

If we're not aware of our belief in specialness and the costs associated with this belief, we continue to pursue a life of being special, at the expense of experiencing universal love and acceptance. Separation is thus perpetuated.

The Unholy Instant

A Course in Miracles

The unholy instant is the starting point of separation and egos giving rise to special relationships housing the mad idea of separation in physical bodies.

> The instant that the mad idea of making your relationship with God unholy [special] seemed to be possible, all your relationships were made meaningless. In that unholy instant time was born, and bodies made to house the mad idea and give it the illusion of reality. And so it seemed to have a home that held together for a little while in time, and vanished.[274]

The body is the ego's idol; the belief in sin made flesh and then projected outward. This produces what seems to be a wall of flesh around the mind, keeping it prisoner in a tiny spot of space and time, beholden unto death, and given but an instant in which to sigh, and grieve and die in honor of its master. And this unholy instant seems to be life; an instant of despair, a tiny island of dry sand, bereft of water and set uncertainly upon oblivion.[275]

The body is the means by which the ego tries to make the unholy relationship seem real. The unholy instant is the time of bodies. But the purpose here is sin [a belief in separation]. It cannot be attained but in illusion, and so the illusion of a brother as body is quite in keeping with the purpose of unholiness.[276]

UNITY

A fairly close [but not exact] parallel passage in Charles Fillmore's writings expresses the idea that taking on material form [that is, bodies] would never have happened if we had not departed from the divine idea of our being, the departure that The Course terms "the unholy instant":

> The Garden of Eden or Paradise of God is in the ether, and we see that the "fall of man" antedated the formation of this planet as we behold it geologically. Jesus recognized this when He said: "And now, Father, glorify thou me with thine own self with the glory which I had with thee before the world was. We are by birth a spiritual race, and we should never have known matter or material conditions if we had followed the leadings of our higher consciousness.[277]

Specialness as a Strategy of the Ego

In the Text of *A Course in Miracles*, Chapter 24 focuses on specialness. Specialness is a strategy of the ego. The ego wishes to *be* special. Originally, it wished for special love from God, which God could not give. The ego, therefore, seeks special love from other people as a substitute for the special love it did not get from God.

Special love is a substitute for Divine Love, which is for all. Specialness is used to perpetuate the belief in separation. In specialness, our use of ego-based judgment becomes more important than the Holy Spirit's answers. It is based on comparisons requiring judgment to make some things special and others not. In specialness some things and/or people are wanted while others are not. Some are included while others are excluded. Some are good, others are bad. Some are important, some are not. And, to the ego, what makes something or someone good and important is that it contributes to the ego's hope for specialness (a sense of rightness or of being right).

A Course in Miracles

Comparison must be an ego device, for love makes none. Specialness always makes comparisons.[278]

Specialness is the function that you gave yourself. It stands for you alone, as self-created, self-maintained, in need of nothing, and unjoined with anything beyond the body. In its eyes you are a separate universe, with all the power to hold itself complete within itself, with every entry shut against intrusion, and every window barred against the light.[279]

Specialness is a lack of trust in anyone except yourself. Faith is invested in yourself alone. Everything else becomes your enemy; feared and attacked, deadly and dangerous, hated and worthy only of destruction. Whatever gentleness it offers is but deception, but its hate is real.[280]

But what is different calls for judgment, and this must come from someone "better," someone incapable of being like what he condemns, "above" it, sinless by comparison with it. ... For specialness not only sets apart, but serves as grounds from which attack on those who seem "beneath" the special one is "natural" and "just." The special ones feel weak and frail because of differences, for what would make them special is their enemy.[281]

Unity

Unity writings have similar things to say about judgment.

> Judging from the plane of the personal leads into condemnation, and condemnation is always followed by the fixing of a penalty. We see faults in others, and pass judgment upon them without considering motives or circumstances. Our judgment is often biased and prejudiced; yet we do not hesitate to think of some form of punishment to be meted out to the guilty one.[282]

Separation and Specialness

A Course in Miracles

Separation and specialness inevitably lead to the loss of peace, hate, anxiety, despair, guilt, attack and pain.

> In looking at the special relationship, it is necessary first to realize that it involves a great amount of pain. Anxiety, despair, guilt

and attack all enter into it, broken into by periods in which they seem to be gone. All these must be understood for what they are. Whatever form they take, they are always an attack on the self to make the other guilty.[283]

The demand for specialness, and the perception of the giving of specialness as an act of love, would make love hateful.[284]

Pursuit of specialness is always at the cost of peace. ... But the pursuit of specialness must bring you pain.[285]

We have said that to limit love to part of the Sonship is to bring guilt into your relationships, and thus make them unreal. If you seek to separate out certain aspects of the totality and look to them to meet your imagined needs, you are attempting to use separation to save you. How, then, could guilt not enter? For separation is the source of guilt, and to appeal to it for salvation is to believe you are alone. To be alone is to be guilty. For to experience yourself as alone is to deny the Oneness of the Father and His Son, and thus attack reality.[286]

Because of guilt, all special relationships have elements of fear in them. This is why they shift and change so frequently. They are not based on changeless love alone. And, love, where fear has entered, cannot be depended on because it is not perfect.[287]

UNITY

Unity writings, published and unpublished, have similar things to say about separation and guilt.

We are all guilty in a way of undue devotion to personal aims, which are always narrow and selfish. So long as these exist and take the place of the rightful One there is no room for the higher self, the Christ of God.[288]

When we hold ourselves in guilt and condemnation, the natural energies of the mind are weakened…. [289]

In other words, you took your share of substance from the Father Mind, and took it away, in a measure. You separated yourself from that substance, and if you carry that to the excess of the part of race consciousness, you develop a sense of separation such that you forget all about the Source; consequently, you are in a state of guilt.[290]

Protection of Specialness

A Course in Miracles

Specialness is essential to the ego:

> It is essential to the preservation of the ego that you believe this specialness is not hell, but Heaven.[291]

Therefore, to the ego, specialness must be defended at any cost.

> All that is ever cherished as a hidden belief, to be defended though unrecognized, is faith in specialness. This takes many forms, but always clashes with the reality of God's creation and with the grandeur He gave His Son….Only the special could have enemies, for they are different and not the same. And difference of any kind imposes orders of reality, and a need to judge that cannot be escaped.[292]

> Those who are special must defend illusions against the truth. For what is specialness but an attack upon the Will of God?[293]

> How bitterly does everyone tied to this world defend the specialness he wants to be the truth! ... Nothing his specialness demands does he withhold. Nothing it needs does he deny to what he loves. ... No effort too great, no cost too much, no price too dear to save his specialness from the least slight, the tiniest attack, the whispered doubt, the hint of threat, or anything but deepest reverence.[294]

Unity also sees conflict between the adverse ego and spiritual consciousness:

> The conflict between Saul and David represents the war in man between the head and the heart, personal will and divine love, for control. The will functioning in sense consciousness would destroy its own soul (Jonathan) and innate love (David).[295]

Special (Unholy) Relationships

A Course in Miracles

An extensive focus on the nature of special relationships is found in chapters 16 through 20 in the Text of *A Course in Miracles*. The special relationship is meant to be a substitute for the Love of God, our True Reality. It maintains that we misuse our special relationships. Believing ourselves to be incomplete and lacking in many respects, we look outside ourselves, to other people, to complete ourselves. These relationships become what it terms "a shabby substitute for what makes you whole in truth, not in illusion."[296]. These are what The Course calls "unholy relationships." It is the aim of The Course to transform all unholy relationships into *holy* relationships, restoring them to their God-given function:

> I have said repeatedly that the Holy Spirit would not deprive you of your special relationships, but would transform them. And all that is meant by that is that He will restore to them the function given them by God.[297]

> The holy relationship, a major step toward the perception of the real world, is learned. It is the old, unholy relationship, transformed and seen anew.[298]

Unholy special relationships are founded on the ego's desire for special love from God. God does not offer such special love because God *is* love and does not distinguish or discriminate. The ego therefore seeks special love elsewhere. It renounces the real, all-encompassing love of God, which refuses to grant it the specialness it desires, and looks to relationship partners to provide the "missing" specialness. Because such relationships are based on a rejection of Reality and an illusion of lack, they inevitably fail to satisfy, leading to an endless search for "the" special relationship."

> It is the special relationship, born of the hidden wish for special love from God, that the ego's hatred triumphs. For the special relationship is the renunciation of the Love of God, and the attempt to secure for the self the specialness that He denied. It is essential to the preservation of the ego that you believe this specialness is not hell, but Heaven. For the ego would never have you see that separation could only be loss, being the one condition in which Heaven could not be.[299]

An unholy relationship is an illusion of a relationship; it only seems to be what it is not. It seems to be joining when, in fact, it is isolating.

> An unholy relationship is no relationship. It is a state of isolation, which seems to be what it is not.[300]

As asserted in the section on the unholy instant, the body has a major role in maintaining special relationships:

> The special relationship is a device for limiting yourself to a body, and for limiting your perception of others to theirs.[301]

> The special relationship is a ritual of form, aimed at raising the form [the body] to take the place of God at the expense of content. There is no meaning in the form, and there never will be. The special relationship must be recognized for what it is: a senseless ritual in which strength is extracted from the death of God, and invested in His killer [the ego, our separated self] as the sign that form has triumphed over content, and love has lost its meaning.[302]

In all likelihood, every relationship we have established in our lives has been based on specialness where something will be acquired or accomplished through the relationship; we believe we have a lack that the other can provide. We are looking outside ourselves to complete ourselves. This might also include giving something of what "I have of lesser value" to gain something of "more value" from the other. While the emphasis of the teachings focuses on relationships with individuals, it also includes relationships with larger groups, organizations, ideas, and even objects.

To give you a sense of the pervasiveness of this topic, people have special relationships with *The Bible*, *A Course in Miracles*, the writings of Charles and Myrtle Fillmore, and any other sacred text. The essential point is the relationship is a means to acquire something that is of value to the ego. Thus unholy special relationships perpetuate separation.

> Any relationship you would substitute for another has not been offered to the Holy Spirit for His use. There *is* no substitute for love. If you would attempt to substitute one aspect of love for another, you have placed less value on one and more on the other. You have not only separated them, but you have also judged

against both. Yet you have judged against yourself first, or you would never have imagined that you needed your brothers as they were not. Unless you had seen yourself as without love, you could not have judged them so like you in lack.[303]

...what is different [what we perceive as different] calls for judgment, and this must come from someone "better," someone incapable of being like what he condemns, "above" it, sinless by comparison with it. And thus does specialness become a means and end at once. For specialness not only sets apart, but serves as grounds from which attack on those who seem "beneath" the special one is "natural" and "just." The special ones feel weak and frail because of differences, for what would make them special *is* their enemy. Yet they protect its enmity and call it "friend." On its behalf they fight against the universe, for nothing in the world they value more.[304]

For an unholy relationship is based on differences, where each one thinks the other has what he has not. They come together, each to complete himself and rob the other. They stay until they think there is nothing left to steal, and then move on. And so they wander through a world of strangers, unlike themselves, living with their bodies perhaps under a common roof that shelters neither; in the same room and yet a world apart.

A holy relationship starts from a different premise. Each one has looked within and seen no lack. Accepting his completion, he would extend it by joining with another, whole as himself. He sees no difference between these selves, for differences are only of the body. Therefore, he looks on nothing he would take. He denies not his own reality because it is the truth.[305]

Ultimately, the teachings demonstrate any special relationship can be the opportunity for the shift to a holy relationship; a means to realize the universality of Love, of God's Love, that is everyone's eternal truth. All manner of relationships as outlined above provide the opportunity for such a shift to a holy relationship.

> In His function as interpreter of what you made, the Holy Spirit uses special relationships, which you have chosen to support the ego, as learning experiences that point to truth. Under His teaching, every relationship becomes a lesson in love.
>
> The Holy Spirit knows no one is special, Yet He also perceives that you have made special relationships, which He would purify and not let you destroy. However unholy the reason you made them may be, He can translate them into holiness by removing as much fear as you will let Him.[306]

Special Hate (Unholy) Relationships

A Course in Miracles

We've come to understand all special relationships are based on hate. They stem from an initial judgment of our self that is based on lack, limit, and insufficiency-essentially self-hatred. That perception is then projected externally, in an attempt to alleviate such personal fear and pain. This is the illusion that develops the "need for special relationships." Further, "special love relationships" appear to be the remedy to the hate and fear we are experiencing. They are, however but a continuation of the same thought system.

> Be not afraid to look upon the special hate relationship, for freedom lies in looking at it. It would be impossible not to know the meaning of love, except for this. For the special love relationship, in which the meaning of love is hidden, is undertaken solely to offset the hate, but not to let it go.[307]

In the unholy relationship, it is not the body of the other with which union is attempted, but the bodies of those who are not there [those from the past]. For even the body of the other, already a severely limited perception of him, is not the central focus as it is, or in entirety. ... Every step taken in the making, the maintaining and the breaking off of the unholy relation-ship is a move toward further fragmentation and unreality.[308]

An unholy relationship is no relationship. It is a state of isolation, which seems to be what it is not. No more than that. The instant that the mad idea of making your relations with God unholy seemed to be possible, all your relationships were made meaningless. In that unholy instant time was born, and bodies made to house the mad idea and give it the illusion of reality. And so it seemed to have a home that held together for a little while in time, and vanished.[309]

SPECIAL LOVE RELATIONSHIPS

A COURSE IN MIRACLES

Special love is based on the past where we taught ourselves that special aspects of the Sonship give us more than others.

> To believe that special relationships, with special love, can offer you salvation is the belief that separation is salvation. ... How can you decide that special aspects of the Sonship can give you more than others? The past has taught you this.[310]

That which we value and believe to be the source of our happiness is referred to as "special love," or "special love relationships." Thus we are striving for an external relationship or matter to "complete" ourselves, to make ourselves happy and whole. The lack thereof we then attribute as the reason for our unhappiness.

> The "better" self the ego seeks is always one that is more special. And whoever seems to possess a special self is "loved" for what can be taken from him. Where both partners see this special self in each other, the ego sees "a union made in Heaven." For neither one will recognize that he asked for hell, and so he will not interfere with the ego's illusion of Heaven, which it offered him to interfere with Heaven.[311]

> The search for the special relationship is the sign that you equate yourself with the ego and not with God. For the special relationship has value only to the ego. To the ego, unless a relationship has special value it has no meaning, for it perceives all love as special. Yet this cannot be natural, for it is unlike the relationship of God and His Son, and all relationships that are unlike this one must be unnatural.[312]

> ...The special love relationship is an attempt to bring love into separation. And, as such, it is nothing more than an attempt to bring love into fear, and make it real in fear.[313]

Special love is merely the illusion of love. All special love relationships hide underlying hatred. The concept of "hatred" here includes all forms of desires to attack another or perceptions of *being attacked* by another. It also includes our efforts to compel our relationship partners to complete us or to make us happy—something that can *only* come from within ourselves, in union with God. Such impossible demands are seen by The Course as attempts to *steal specialness* from the other.

> The special love relationship is the ego's most boasted gift, and one which has the most appeal to those unwilling to relinquish guilt. ... Here they [the fantasies about special love] are usually

judged to be acceptable and even natural. No one considers it bizarre to love and hate together, and even those who believe that hate is sin merely feel guilty, but do not correct it. This is the "natural" condition of the separation... Here, where the illusion of love is accepted in love's place, love is perceived as separation and exclusion.[314]

Time is indeed unkind to the unholy relationship. ...The attraction of the unholy relationship begins to fade and to be questioned almost at once. Once it is formed, doubt must enter in, because its purpose is impossible. The "ideal" of the unholy relationship thus becomes one in which the reality of the other does not enter at all to "spoil" the dream. And the less the other really brings to the relationship, the "better" it becomes. Thus the attempt at union becomes a way of excluding even the one with whom the union was sought. For it [the relationship] was formed to get him out of it, and join with fantasies in uninterrupted "bliss."[315]

For the special love relationship, in which the meaning of love is hidden, is undertaken solely to offset the hate, but not to let it go. ... You cannot limit hate. The special love relationship will not offset it. But will merely drive it underground and out of sight. [316]

The special love relationship is an attempt to limit the destructive effects of hate by finding a haven in the storm of guilt. It makes no attempt to rise above the storm, into the sunlight. ... The special love relationship is not perceived as a value in itself, but as a place of safety from which hatred is split off and kept apart. The special love partner is acceptable only as long as he serves this purpose. Hatred can enter, and indeed is welcome in some aspects of the relationship, but it is still held together by the illusion of love. If the illusion goes, the relationship is broken or becomes unsatisfying on the grounds of disillusionment.[317]

Unity

While Unity does not focus on relationships as the primary spiritual classroom, it does have some things to say about the need to rise above our usual conceptions about our relationships.

> So the I AM that desires to function on the spiritual plane must drop all belief in fleshly parentage. It must count as rubbish all pride of ancestry and "blue blood."...This form of human pride must be denied as a dream of the night, because it is one of the strong cords that bind the I AM to the flesh. Every tie of earthly relationship must be recognized as the passing condition of a brief fleshly experience. Your children are not yours as you have looked upon them. They are egos like yourself, through some similarity of desire they have been attracted to your mental stratum...You will love them with a love that will help to lift them into the eternal heaven when you know that they are not yours alone, but that all men and women compose one great common family with God as the Father-Mother.[318]

> Selfishness has its stronghold in the personal man's claims upon the things that he loves. No one was ever permanently satisfied with personal love. Some of its fruit is bitter and its end is death. This may seem a hard saying, but it is true, and we might as well awaken at once to the love universal, in which is perfect satisfaction.[319]

> Love is not selfish. We cannot have selfishness and love at the same time. We cannot have this universal brotherhood unless we love everybody. We must love all because we are all one. There must be in our consciousness a recognition of the universal right of all to all the possessions of the world.[320]

Myrtle Fillmore, in letters to various individuals, had words of wisdom for people in family relationships, particularly about seeing past the personality (ego) to the Christ within. Our interactions are part of what we are learning and extending outward to include "all humanity:" Our interactions become the means to learn to extend love to all humanity.

> Let's not condemn ourselves or resent it if at times a dear one feels a spurt of ambition or anxiety, or fails to see things just as we do. Let's endeavor to look through the veil of personality and see the Christ within, and trust this God-self to come through, gloriously![321]

> Now, dear, just turn your entire attention to God and earnestly seek to see as He sees. See your children as eagerly growing souls. See them as individuals unfolding their own faculties and powers, individually doing that which seems to them best at the moment... Be not only willing but happy to think of your children and all others as they are in God's kingdom—free, free to live life as they see it—free to change, where they feel they have made mistakes, or where the present mode of living seems to depress or to hinder progress—free to stand for their highest ideals, assured of blessings from others.[322]

> The love that is the fulfilling of the law is not the personal affection and the clinging to personality that is the usual expression of a happily mated man and woman. Love that fulfills the law is the great sense of unity that prompts the soul to seek the understanding and practice of that which is for the welfare not only of the beloved but of all humanity.[323]

SUMMARY

This chapter presents the significance of specialness as it relates to our lives and our world. The root of the "world's" form of specialness is what makes me different and better (or worse) than others; what makes me more (or less) important, valuable, attractive, successful, etc. The striving for specialness also requires being in a constant state of judgment towards our self and others. For one to "be successful," another must not. And here is the opportunity for awakening. There is nothing that the Holy Spirit will not use to heal. Whatever form of ego specialness we initiate can ultimately be a tool of the Holy Spirit in our mind; our tool for separation becomes a means for our transformation. Chapter 7 explores how relationships become our salvation rather than our doom.

CHAPTER 7

The Holy Instant, The Holy Relationship

INTRODUCTION

In *A Course in Miracles*, specialness is no minor aspect of our illusion. Our ego strives to have us believe our specialness in the world is what gives our life meaning. If we do not feel special, where do we turn for help? The ego. If we do feel special, how do we perpetuate this? The ego. And what are the results? Most likely, more of the same- separation, fear, and aloneness. The relinquishment of all of the world's forms of specialness paves the way to our awakening.

To deal with separation, which The Course calls the only problem, The Course introduces the Holy Spirit's means of addressing specialness- the holy instant and the holy relationship. When we are ready and willing, we question the nature of our "specialness" or "special relationships," and we find the answers. In the holy instant we experience the reality of love; we also find mistaken beliefs discarded, but a faint memory of a past error remains.

There is nothing in published Unity materials about The Course's topics of special relationships, holy relationships or holy instants. However, material on the importance of healing broken relationships through forgiveness can be found. In addition, the importance of moving from limited ideas of love to universal love can be found as well as moving from limited man to Christ man.

The Holy Instant

The purpose of the holy instant is to suspend judgment by freeing us from the past. It reflects God's timeless Knowledge. In the holy instant we have an instant of clarity when we experience a completely different state of being. In that instant we remember unity.

A Course in Miracles.

> The holy instant is the Holy Spirit's most useful learning device for teaching you love's meaning. For its purpose is to suspend judgment entirely. [324]

> God knows you now. He remembers nothing, having always known you exactly as He knows you now. The holy instant reflects His knowing by bringing all perception out of the past, thus removing the frame of reference you have built by which to judge your brothers. Once this is gone, the Holy Spirit substitutes His frame of reference for it. His frame of reference is simply God. The Holy Spirit's timelessness lies only here. For in the holy instant, free of the past, you see that love is in you, and you have no need to look without and snatch love guiltily from where you thought it was. [325]

> Yet in the holy instant you unite directly with God, and all your brothers join in Christ. Those who are joined in Christ are in no way separate. For Christ is the Self the Sonship shares, as God shares His Self with Christ. [326]

> In the holy instant no one is special, for your personal needs intrude on no one to make your brothers seem different [327]

> The holy relationship is the expression of the holy instant in living in this world. ... The holy relationship is a constant reminder

of the experience in which the relationship became what it is. And as the unholy relationship is a continuing hymn of hate in praise of its maker [the ego], so is the holy relationship a happy song of praise to the Redeemer [the Holy Spirit] of relationships.[328]

UNITY

In Unity writings on the importance of the oneness of the Sonship through the Christ can be found. There is a definite emphasis on seeing the Christ in all of humanity.

> Sonship in Christ is the goal… We are endeavoring to see the Christ in all humanity, and to call attention to and encourage the development of the Christ in all who are receptive. We are assured that the Christ Mind in us is working in our consciousness to cast out all that does not measure up. [329]

> Jesus recognized divine sonship and universal brotherhood. We confess Jesus as the Son of God, and by that confession we acknowledge that all men [people] are sons of God.[330]

> sonship—Man [humankind], through Christ within, is God's son. Man reveals his sonship to himself and to others by claiming it; by declaring that he is not a son of mortality but a son of God; that the Spirit of God dwells within him and shines through him; that this Spirit is Christ, Son of God. [331]

THE HOLY SPIRIT AND YOUR "SPECIAL FUNCTION"

The Holy Spirit uses the specialness we made—even our special love relationships—to fulfill the true function of salvation. The Holy Spirit guides us to correct the specialness where the error lies, in our mind.

Holding on to past grievances prevents the light of the Holy Spirit from entering our minds. In the holy instant the meaning of Real Love is realized through letting go of the past by the suspension of judgment resulting in forgiveness.

A Course in Miracles

My grievances hide the light of the world in me.[332]

The Holy Spirit serves Christ's purpose in your mind, so that the aim of specialness can be corrected where the error lies. [333]

Such is the Holy Spirit's kind perception of specialness; His use of what you made, to heal instead of harm. To each [person] He gives a special function in salvation he [the person] alone can fill; a part for only him.[334]

The Holy Spirit needs your special function, that His may be fulfilled. Think not you lack a special value here. You wanted it, and it is given you. All that you made can serve salvation easily. [335]

Only in darkness does your specialness appear to be attack. In light, you see it as your special function in the plan to save the Son of God from all attack, and let him understand that he is safe, as he has always been, and will remain in time and in eternity alike. This is the function given you for your brother. [336]

The specialness he chose to hurt himself did God appoint to be the means for his salvation, from the very instant that the choice was made. His special sin was made his special grace. His special hate became his special [universal] love.[337]

Unity

While Unity does not refer to the holy instant or the holy relationship, the Holy Spirit is a key component in overcoming the judgment, condemnation and unjust ways of humankind engendered by the adverse ego. The reader will quickly perceive the similarity in the *concepts* between the Unity quotes below and the *A Course in Miracles* quotes above.

> The Holy Spirit is the "outpouring" or activity of the living word. The work of the Holy Spirit is the executive power of Father (mind) and Son (idea), carrying out the creative plan. It is through the help of the Holy Spirit that man overcomes. The Holy Spirit reveals, helps, and directs in this overcoming. The work that the overcomer does for the world is to help establish a new race consciousness, "new heavens and a new earth, wherein dwelleth righteousness." By being true to his highest understanding of Truth the overcomer never swerves to the right nor left for any reason.[338]

> If you think that you are unjustly treated by your friends, your employers, your government, or those with whom you do business, simply declare the activity of the almighty Mind [The Holy Spirit], and you will set into action mental forces that will find expression in the executors of the law. This is the most lasting reform to which man can apply himself. It is much more effective than legislation or any attempt to control unjust men by human ways.[339]

> The remedy for all that appears unjust is denial of condemnation of others, or of self, and affirmation of the great universal Spirit of justice, through which all unequal and unrighteous conditions are finally adjusted.
>
> Observing the conditions that exist in the world, the just man would have them righted according to what he perceives to be the equitable law. ... Jesus gave this treatment for such a mental

condition: "For neither doth the Father judge any man, but he hath given all judgment unto the Son." This Son is the Christ, the Universal cosmos; to its equity, man should commit the justice that he wishes to see brought into human affairs. Put all the burdens of the world upon the one supreme Judge and hold every man, and all the conditions in which men are involved, amenable to the law of God. By so doing, you will set into action mind forces powerful and far-reaching.[340]

The Holy Relationship

We are always in the holy relationship though not in our conscious awareness. The holy relationship reflects God's purpose, which is based on loving all of God's Sons equally. The resolution of specialness arises from our realizing every person's ultimate goal is the same - realizing true, divine love and holiness. The unholy special relationship is transformed into the holy relationship. A holy relationship sees no differences, no specialness. In the holy relationship, the body has no function.

A Course in Miracles

The holy relationship is the expression of the holy instant in living in this world.[341]

The holy relationship, a major step toward the perception of the real world, is learned. It is the old, unholy relationship, transformed and seen anew. The holy relationship is a phenomenal teaching accomplishment. In all its aspects, as it begins, develops and comes accomplished, it represents the reversal of the unholy relationship. Be comforted in this; the only difficult phase is the beginning. For here, the goal of the relationship is abruptly shifted to the exact opposite of what it was. This is the first result of offering the relationship to the Holy Spirit, to use for His purposes. [342]

You are forever in a relationship so holy that it calls to everyone to escape from loneliness, and join you in your love.[343]

You cannot enter into real relationships with any of God's Sons unless you love them all and equally. Love is not special.[344]

Would it be possible for you to hate your brother if you were like him? Could you attack him if you realized you journey with him, to a goal that is the same? ...
    Your brother is your friend because his Father created him like you. There is no difference. You have been given to your brother that love might be extended, not cut off from him. ... God gave you and your brother Himself, and to remember this is now the only purpose you share. And so it is the only one you have. [345]

Your brother's body is as little use to you as it is to him. When it [the body] is used only as the Holy Spirit teaches, it has no function. For minds need not the body to communicate. The sight that sees the body has no use which serves the purpose of a holy relationship. [346]

UNITY

While Unity does not address holy relationships, it agrees that every person shares the same spiritual goal - coming "into the consciousness of an indwelling God," the I AM. Limited love must be transformed into universal love. Personal man must be transformed into universal man, the Christ man. Relationships must be healed if we, as individuals, are to be healed.

The ultimate aim of every man should be to come into the consciousness of an indwelling God, and then, in all external matters, to affirm deliverance through and by this Divine One.[347]

The I AM is the same in all men and all women. It is without limit in its capacity to express the potentialities of God.[348]

Just to the extent that we separate ourselves into families, cliques, and religious factions we put away God's love. Unless there is specific denial along every line of human-thought bondage, one will still be under the law of sense.[349]

… our love goes through a transformation, which broadens, strengthens, and deepens it. We no longer confine love to family, friends, and personal relations, but expand it to include all things. The denial of human relationships seems at first glance to be a repudiation of the family group, but it is merely a cleansing of the mind from limited ideas of love when this faculty would satisfy itself solely by means of human kinship. If God is the Father of all, then men and women are brothers and sisters in a universal family, and he who sees spiritually should open his heart and cultivate that inclusive love which God has given as the unifying element in the human family. [350]

The personal man with all his limitations, all his relations, must give way to the universal, the Christ man. The privilege is ours to give up or forsake everything--father, mother, husband, wife, children, houses, lands--for Christ's sake and so enter into the consciousness of eternal life. By doing this we come into the realization of eternal life and receive a hundredfold more of the very things that we have forsaken. If we refuse or neglect to make this "sacrifice" and prefer to live in the narrow, personal way, and cling to the old personal relationships, there is nothing for it but to meet the result of our choice, and to sever all those relations by death. It is just a question of giving up a little for the all and gaining eternal life. [351]

Forgiveness and the Holy Relationship

Forgiveness re-establishes the awareness of the Holy Relationship. It is our willingness to use the Holy Spirit that translates specialness into salvation. Through forgiveness we recognize that we are all "special," which is the means of undoing the ego's kind of specialness. Forgiveness enables me to realize that my salvation is identical to my brother's.

A Course in Miracles

> The specialness of God's Sons does not stem from exclusion but from inclusion. All my brothers are special. [352]

> The holiness of your relationship forgives you and your brother, undoing the effects of what you both believe and saw. [353]

> It [the holy relationship] is the old, unholy relationship, transformed and seen anew. ... In all its aspects, as it begins, develops and becomes accomplished, it represents the reversal of the unholy relationship. ...
> For once the unholy relationship has accepted the goal of holiness, it can never again be what it was.[354]

> Forgiveness is the end of specialness. Only illusions can be forgiven, and they disappear. Forgiveness is release from all illusions, and this is why it is impossible but partly to forgive.[355]

> Forgiveness is the only function meaningful in time. It is the means the Holy Spirit uses to translate specialness from sin into salvation. Forgiveness is for all. ... Yet while in time, there is still much to do. And each must do what is allotted him, for on his part does all the plan depend. He has a special part in time for so he chose, and choosing it, he made it for himself. His wish was not

denied but changed in form, to let it serve his brother and himself, and thus become a means to save instead of lose.[356]

Unity

In Unity, unforgiveness and resentment keeps us in our limited selves and separate from others. Love, seeing good, and forgiveness removes all discord and discomfort.

> You may trust love to get you out of your difficulties. There is nothing too hard for it to accomplish for you, if you put your confidence in it and act without dissimulation. But do not talk love and in your heart feel resentment. This will bring discord to your members and rottenness to your bones. Love is candor and frankness. Deception is no part of love; he who tries to use it in that sort of company will prove himself a liar, and love will desert him in the end.
>
> There is no envy in love. Love is satisfaction in itself, not that satisfaction with personal self, its possessions and its attractions, which is vanity, but an inner satisfaction that sees good everywhere and in everybody. It insists that all is good, and by refusing to see anything but good it causes that quality finally to appear uppermost in itself and in all things. When only good is seen and felt, how can there be anything but satisfaction?[357]

> We must forgive as we would be forgiven. To forgive does not simply mean to arrive at a place of indifference to those who do personal injury to us; it means far more than this. To forgive is to give for--to give some actual, definite good in return for evil given. One may say: "I have no one to forgive; I have not a personal enemy in the world." And yet if, under any circumstances, any kind of a "served-him-right" thought springs up within you over anything that any of God's children may do or suffer, you have not yet learned how to forgive.

The very pain that you suffer, the very failure to demonstrate over some matter that touches your own life deeply, may rest upon just this spirit of unforgiveness that you harbor toward the world in general. Put it away with resolution.

Do not be under bondage to false beliefs about your circumstances or environment. No matter how evil circumstances may appear, or how much it may seem that some other personality is at the foundation of your sorrow or trouble, God, good, good alone, is really there when you call His law into expression.

If we have the courage to persist in seeing only God in it all, even "the wrath of man" (Ps. 76:10) shall be invariably turned to our advantage. Joseph, in speaking of the action of his brethren in selling him into slavery, said, "As for you, ye meant evil against me; but God meant it for good" (Gen. 50:20). To them that love God, "all things work together for good" (Rom. 8:28), or to them who recognize only God. All things! The very circumstances in your life that seem heartbreaking evils will turn to joy before your very eyes if you will steadfastly refuse to see anything but God in them. [358]

Forgiveness is not silent consent, the negative appearance of making the best of a situation while underneath there is resentment. Forgiveness is the art of putting something else in place of the thing forgiven. You put the positive realization of the Truth of Being in place of the appearance of negation and adversity which your senses and your intellectual training report. It does not matter that there is no immediate transformation; you have made use of your God power to erase the appearance and to establish Truth. Such an attitude invites only the best from other souls.[359]

CHAPTER 8

Love and Fear, Sin, Guilt and Judgment

—⚏—

LOVE AND FEAR

LOVE AND FEAR IS AN important duality worth exploring from the perspective of *A Course in Miracles* and Unity. Both systems say that fear is dependent upon the Divine (Love) for its existence. Fear masks or hides Love from awareness. Both teachings see love as what is Real and permanent while fear is unreal and temporary. The awareness and experience of Love's presence dispels fear.

A Course in Miracles

In *A Course in Miracles*, love is an essential aspect of the teaching. It specifically states,

> The *Course* does not aim at teaching the true meaning of love, for that is beyond what can be taught. It does aim, however, at removing the blocks to the awareness of love's presence, which is your natural inheritance.[360]

Students of *A Course in Miracles* learn love is real and fear is an illusion. The essence of our reality is Love; our existence as God's Creation, God's extension, is love. Whenever we are not experiencing love, we are applying our conscious thoughts towards an illusion.

> I have said you have but two emotions, love and fear. One [love] is changeless but continually exchanged, being offered by the eternal to the eternal…The other [fear] has many forms for the content of individual illusions differs greatly. Yet they have one thing in common; they are all insane.[361]

> The opposite of love is fear, but what is all encompassing can have no opposite.[362]

The entire purpose of *A Course in Miracles* is twofold:

(1) Discover and remove "all blocks to the awareness of love's presence" – the fear-based belief system we accept and live.
(2) Deepen our awareness of love as our Reality, our state of Being.

> For this is a course on love, because it is about you.[363]

This first step calls for the undoing of ego-based beliefs, essentially our belief in separation and the fear it engenders.

> Fear and love are the only emotions of which you are capable. One is false, for it [fear] was made out of denial; and denial depends on the belief in what is denied [love] for its [fear's] own existence. By interpreting fear correctly as a positive affirmation of the underlying belief [love] it [fear] masks, you are undermining its [fear's] perceived usefulness and rendering it [fear] useless.[364]

Here are some other ways love and fear are described in *A Course in Miracles* itself.

Healing is a way of forgetting the sense of danger the ego has induced in you, by not recognizing its existence in your brother. This strengthens the Holy Spirit in both of you, because it is a refusal to acknowledge fear. Love needs only this invitation. It comes freely to all the Sonship, being what the Sonship is. By your awakening to it, you are merely forgetting what you are not. This enables you to remember what you are.[365]

Mind always reproduces as it was produced. Produced by fear, the ego reproduces fear. This is its allegiance, and this allegiance makes it treacherous to your love because you are love. Love is your power, which the ego must deny.[366]

You are afraid of this [living without ego judgment] because you believe that without the ego, all would be chaos. Yet I assure you that without the ego, all would be love.[367]

UNITY

In Unity writings, it can be inferred that fear is dependent upon love. When we focus on love, fear is cast out of consciousness.

Fear--Fear is one of the most subtle and destructive errors that the carnal mind in man experiences. Fear is a paralyzer of mental action; it weakens both mind and body. Fear throws dust in our eyes and hides the mighty spiritual forces that are always with us. Blessed are those who deny ignorance and fear and affirm the presence and power of Spirit.[368]

The one and only remedy for the crosscurrents of fear is the restoration of the peace and harmony of life by love and its combinations.[369]

Fear, how to overcome--Fear is cast out by perfect love. To know divine love is to be selfless, and to be selfless is to be without fear.[370]

SIN AND THE CORRECTION OF SIN

Traditionally, sin is viewed as a transgression against the law of God and therefore against God. In this sense, sin is punishable by God. Both *A Course in Miracles* and Unity take a different view from this traditional view. To them both, the traditional view is error thinking. We are not punished "for our sins" but "by our sins" and not by God. In a deeper sense, sin would be any thought or feeling that supports the erroneous belief in separation.

A Course in Miracles

The basic sin or error is the substitution of illusion for Truth.

> Sin is the belief in the reality of our separation from God... sin is the equivalent to separation, ... to the Holy Spirit, sins are errors to be corrected and healed.[371]

> You who believe that God is fear made but one substitution. It has taken many forms because it was the substitute of illusion for truth; ... It has become so splintered and subdivided and divided again, over and over, that it is now almost impossible to perceive it once was one, and still is what it was. That one error, which brought truth to illusion, infinity to time, and life to death, was all you ever made. Your whole world rests upon it. Everything you see reflects it, and every special relationship that you have ever made is part of it.[372]

> But nothing you have seen begins to show you the enormity of [this] original error, which seemed to cast you out of Heaven, to shatter your knowledge into meaningless bits of disunited perceptions, and to force you to make further substitutions.[373]

> That was the first projection of error outward. The world arose to hide it, and became the screen on which it was projected, and drawn between you and the truth. …Call it not sin but madness, for such it was and so it still remains.[374]

Ultimately, since what we call "sin" is merely an error that needs correction, The Course strongly asserts that there is no such thing as sin:

> There is no sin; it has no consequence.[375]

> If sin is real, then punishment is just and cannot be escaped.[376]

Correction of Sin (A Course in Miracles)
Sin is an error belief, waiting to be corrected/forgiven. *A Course in Miracles'* description of the error (the belief in separation) which has been believed to be a sin is not eternal. It is not real.

> The Son of God could never sin, but he can wish for what would hurt him. And he has the power to think he can be hurt. What could this be except a misperception of himself? Is this a sin or a mistake, forgivable or not? … Make then your choice. But recognize that in this choice the purpose of the world you see is chosen, and will be justified.[377]

> You see it [sin] still, because you do not realize that its foundation has gone. Its source [the substitution of illusion for Truth] has

been removed, and so it can be cherished but a little while before it vanishes.

…You will be healed of sin and all its ravages the instant that you give it no power over your brother.[378]

We are the ones who need to make the correction because we are the ones who made the mistake. We choose the Love of God, and we release any belief in sin.

Before a holy relationship there is no sin. The form of error is no longer seen, and reason, joined with love, looks quietly on all confusion, observing merely, "This was a mistake."[379]

UNITY

Unity agrees that, ultimately, sin is unreal; sin is error or missing the mark. It is a result of not realizing our Divinity (Christ Nature) resulting in a sense of separation and apartness. When we sin we fail to express our Divine Qualities and we fall short of Divine Law. Like in *A Course in Miracles*, sin is correctable.

sin--Missing the mark; that is, falling short of divine perfection. Sin is man's failure to express the attributes of Being--life, love, intelligence, wisdom, and the other God qualities.[380]

Sin and the consciousness of sin are the cause of all darkness and death.[381]

In denying the reality of sin send out your freeing thought to others as well as to yourself. Do not hold anyone in bondage to the thought of sin. If you do, it will pile up and increase in power according to the laws of mental action.[382]

There is no power and no reality in sin. If sin were real and enduring like goodness and Truth, it could not be forgiven but would hold its victim forever.[383]

Correction for Sin (Unity)

Sin (error) is first in mind and is redeemed by a mental process, or by going into the silence. Error is brought into the light of Spirit and then transformed into a constructive force.[384]

Sin is the falling short of divine law, and repentance and forgiveness are the only means that man has of getting out of sin and its effect and coming into harmony with the law.[385]

Sin is a missing of the mark, and we miss the mark by not having faith.[386]

Faith in the reality, power, and willingness of the mental and spiritual forces is absolutely essential to success in demonstrating the higher law.[387]

GUILT

A Course in Miracles has a lot more to say about guilt than the Unity writings. In this context, guilt is the judgment of responsibility for having done something wrong and the feelings of remorse and regret associated with it. It is both the judgement and the resulting feeling. We expect punishment, hence we are afraid. Actually, guilt is a condition of relying on an ego based thought system, perpetuated by a fearful state of mind. Therefore, Guilt perpetuates fear.

A Course in Miracles

The Course focuses on the underlying psychology of guilt. . Because of our separation-based thinking, we believe we have sinned against God and will be punished by God. We judge ourselves, and fearfully believe God judges us in the same way. Guilt is an imbedded effect of our thought system driving the fear of such punishment. The interaction of our thoughts of sin-guilt-fear has been referred to as "the un-holy trinity" by Dr. Kenneth Wapnick. The guilt and fear are so uncomfortable that we make the world, other people, and even daily activities responsible for them. This is called projection, and it is an ineffective means to get rid of and avoid facing our guilt, fear, and associated discomfort.

> If the ego is the symbol of the separation, it is also the symbol of guilt. Guilt is more than merely not of God. It is the symbol of attack on God.[388]

Chapter 13 of *A Course in Miracles* is entitled "The Guiltless World." Aspects of the introduction provide valuable insight into the perception of a fearful and punishing God leading to the development of guilt in our thinking.

> …it is guilt that has obscured the Father to you, and it is guilt that has driven you insane.
>
> The acceptance of guilt into the mind of God's Son was the beginning of the separation, as the acceptance of the Atonement is its end. The world you see is the delusional system of those made mad by guilt. Look carefully at this world, and you will realize this is so. For this world is the symbol of punishment, and all the laws that seem to govern it are the laws of death. … Not one of them [all separated sons] but has the thought that God is cruel.

> If this were the real world, God would be cruel. ... Only the world of guilt could demand this, for only the guilty could conceive of it.[389]

> If you identify with the ego, you must perceive yourself as guilty. Whenever you respond to your ego you will experience guilt, and you will fear punishment.
> ...Guilt is a sure sign that your thinking is unnatural. Unnatural thinking will always be attended with guilt, because it is a belief in sin.[390]

> Whenever you are not wholly joyous, it is because you have reacted with a lack of love to one of God's creations. Perceiving this as "sin" you become defensive because you expect attack. The decision to react in this way is yours, and can therefore be undone. It cannot be undone by repentance in the usual sense, because this implies guilt. If you allow yourself to feel guilty, you will reinforce the error rather than allow it to be undone for you.[391]

There is hope in the midst of this guilt:

> Little child, this [our ego-based belief in guilt] is not so. Your "guilty secret" is nothing, and if you will but bring it to the light, the light will dispel it. And then no dark cloud will remain between you and the remembrance of your Father, for you will remember His guiltless Son [Your Self], who did not die because he is immortal.[392]

> The idea that the guiltless Son of God can attack himself and make himself guilty is insane. In any form, in anyone, *believe this not*. For sin and condemnation are the same, and the belief in one is faith in the other, calling for punishment instead of love. Nothing can justify insanity, and to call for punishment upon yourself must be insane.

See no one, then, as guilty, and you will affirm the truth of guiltlessness unto yourself. In every condemnation that you offer the Son of God lies the conviction of your own guilt. If you would have the Holy Spirit make you free of it, accept His offer of Atonement for all your brothers. For so you learn that it is true for you. Remember always that it is impossible to condemn the Son of God in part. Those whom you see as guilty become the witnesses to guilt in you, and you will see it there, for it *is* there until it is undone. Guilt is always in your mind, which has condemned itself. Project it not, for while you do, it cannot be undone.[393]

"Only you can deprive yourself of anything. Do not oppose this realization, for it is truly the beginning of the dawn of light. Remember also that the denial of this simple fact takes many forms, and these you must learn to recognize and to oppose steadfastly, without exception. This is a crucial step in the reawakening. The beginning phases of this reversal are often quite painful, for as blame [projection of guilt] is withdrawn from without, there is a strong tendency to harbor it within. It is difficult at first to realize that this is exactly the same thing, for there is no distinction between within and without.

If your brothers are part of you and you blame them for your deprivation, you are blaming yourself. And you cannot blame yourself without blaming them. That is why blame must be undone, not seen elsewhere.[394]

UNITY

While there is little discussion on guilt in the Unity writings, what it says is very similar to what *A Course in Miracles* teaches. Guilt arises as the effect of focusing on our selfish, personal aims (separation thinking) taking the place of our higher Self. Essentially, guilt also stems from forgetting that God is our Source of Substance.

The Unity view is exemplified in the story of the Prodigal Son (Luke 15:11-32) who took his share of his inheritance, went away, and squandered it. When he realized his error, he felt guilty. It is good to remind ourselves that Substance is the sum total of all Divine Ideas when we read the quote below. Essentially, we believe we took our "rightful Substance" from God and separated ourselves from the remaining Substance of God.

We are all guilty in a way of undue devotion to personal aims, which are always narrow and selfish. So long as these exist and take the place of the rightful One there is no room for the higher self, the Christ of God.[395]

You could not have been made by this infinite Mind and been perfect without your cooperation. You are an identity in yourself. How did you attain that identity of yourself? By expressing the potentialities of Being. In other words, you took your share of substance from the Father Mind, and took it away, in a measure. You separated yourself from that substance, and if you carry that to the excess of the part of race consciousness, you develop a sense of separation such that you forget all about the Source; consequently, you are in a state of guilt. If you are not perpetually, drawing from the Father Mind, you will find eventually there will be a famine in your country. You will have a lack of vigor, vitality, energy, and life.[396]

JUDGMENT

Both *A Course in Miracles* and Unity agree with the biblical admonition to not judge others. They agree judgment can be put to good use in this relative realm. However, *A Course in Miracles* and Unity clearly disagree on whether judgment is an attribute of God or not.

On another level, one can see Unity often uses wisdom as a synonym for judgment, *A Course in Miracles* agrees. *A Course in Miracles* teaches we use the wisdom of God by asking the Holy Spirit for help. Unity teaches that we need to use judgment from the level of the Absolute/God-Mind. In this sense, while *A Course in Miracles* clearly states that wisdom is not judgment, its use of wisdom is very similar to what Unity teaches. In both cases it is the Holy Spirit that provides the right use of judgment.

A Course in Miracles

A Course in Miracles teaches that judgment is not an attribute of God. It is an attribute of the ego that can be put to a useful purpose. In some places, *A Course in Miracles* clearly states that wisdom is an attribute of God and not an attribute of the separated ego mind.

> Judgment is not an attribute of God. It was brought into being only after the separation, when it became one of the many learning devices ... .[397]

> Watch your mind carefully for any beliefs that hinder its accomplishment [the shining away of the ego], and step away from them. Judge how well you have done this by your own feelings, for this is the one right use of judgment. Judgment, like any other kind of defense, can be used to attack or protect; hurt or heal. The ego should be brought to judgment and found wanting there. ... Let it be judged truly and you must withdraw allegiance, protection and love from it.[398]

While two of the next examples do not use the word, judgment, clearly judgment is used to decide between crucifixion and resurrection for ourselves and between crucifixion and redemption for others.

> Each day, each hour and minute, even every second, you are deciding between the crucifixion and the resurrection; between the ego and the Holy Spirit. ...The power of decision is all that is yours. What you can decide between is fixed, because there are no alternatives except truth or illusion.[399]

Each one you see you place within the holy circle of Atonement or leave outside, judging him fit for crucifixion or for redemption. If you bring him into the circle of purity, you will rest there with him. If you leave him without, you join him there.[400]

It is necessary for the teacher of God to realize, not that he should not judge, but that he cannot. In giving up judgment, he is merely giving up what he did not have. He gives up an illusion; or better, he has an illusion of giving up. He has actually merely become more honest. Recognizing that judgment was always impossible for him, he no longer attempts it. This is no sacrifice. On the contrary, he puts himself in a position where judgment *through* him rather than *by* him can occur. And this judgment is neither "good" nor "bad." It is the only judgment there is, and it is only one: "God's Son is guiltless, and sin does not exist."[401]

The Course teaches that the Holy Spirit leads us through a judging or sorting out process with the eventual goal of freeing us from judgment entirely:

The Holy Spirit does not teach you to judge others, because He does not want you to teach error and learn it yourself. He would hardly be consistent if He allowed you to strengthen what you must learn to avoid. In the mind of the thinker, then, He *is* judgmental, but only in order to unify the mind so it can perceive without judgment. This enables the mind to teach without judgment, and therefore to learn to *be* without judgment.[402]

Here is what *A Course in Miracles* has to say about wisdom.

Wisdom is not judgment; it is the relinquishment of judgment.[403]

Innocence is wisdom because it is unaware of evil, and evil does not exist.[404]

It is not until their innocence becomes a viewpoint with universal application that it becomes wisdom.[405]

Say to the Holy Spirit only, "Decide for me," and it is done. ... Learn of His wisdom and His Love, and teach His answer to everyone who struggles in the dark.[406]

Place the ideas within your mind, and let it use them as it chooses. Give it faith that it will use them wisely, being helped in its decision by the One Who gave the thoughts to you. What can you trust but what is in your mind? Have faith, in these reviews, the means the Holy Spirit uses will not fail. The wisdom of your mind [from the Holy Spirit] will come to your assistance.[407]

UNITY

While there are the basic common admonitions about judging others, Unity also teaches we each have the Power of Judgment or Wisdom. It is our innate ability to judge, discern, evaluate and compare. We can judge from our limited ego and sense consciousness or from Higher Consciousness, the Absolute. The latter is what The Course refers to as judgment *through* us rather than *by* us.

> judgment seat--The "judgment-seat" (Rom. 14:10) is within man. A judging, or discerning between the true and the false, is going on daily in us as overcomers; we are daily reaping the results of our thoughts and our deeds.[408]

> Good judgment, like all other faculties of the mind, is developed from Principle. In its perfection it is expressed through man's mind, with all its absolute relations uncurtailed. ... .[409]

The metaphysician finds it necessary to place his judgment in the Absolute in order to demonstrate its supreme power. This is accomplished by one's first declaring that one's judgment is spiritual and not material; that its origin is in God; that all its conclusions are based on Truth and that they are absolutely free from prejudice, false sympathy, or personal ignorance.[410]

…. This is the stand which everyone must take--resting judgment of others in the Absolute. When this is done the tendency to condemn will grow less and less, until man, seeing his fellow man as God sees him, will leave him to the Absolute in all cases where he seems unjust.[411]

The Last Judgment or Judgment Day

A Course in Miracles and Unity hold similar views on the last judgment or judgment day. It is not some final judgment of God against individuals or humankind because God eternally "sees us" as whole and perfect. It is an ongoing process of the right evaluation of and by humankind. The following quotes are self-explanatory.

A Course in Miracles

The Last Judgment might be called a process of right evaluation. It simply means that everyone will finally come to understand what is worthy and what is not. After this, the ability to choose can be directed rationally.[412]

You who believed God's Last Judgment would condemn the world to hell along with you, accept this holy truth: God's Judgment is the gift of the correction He bestowed on all your errors, freeing you from them, and all effects they ever seemed to have.[413]

When *A Course in Miracles* speaks of the Last Judgment, or the Final Judgment, one can understand the "Last Judgment" is the only "Judgment" that has ever been:

> This is God's Final Judgment: "You are still My holy Son, forever innocent, forever loving and forever loved, as limitless as your Creator, and completely changeless and forever pure. Therefore awaken and return to Me. I am your Father and you are My Son.[414]

In the Manual for Teachers, the message is consistent. However the direction called for speaks to our role:

> *Holy are you, eternal, free and whole, at peace forever in the Heart of God. Where is the world, and where is sorrow now?*
> ...Do you believe that this is wholly true? No; not yet, not yet. But this is still your goal; why you are here. It is your function to prepare yourself to hear this Judgment and to recognize that it is true. One instant of complete belief in this, and you will go beyond belief to Certainty. One instant out of time can bring time's end.
> ... It is your function to make that end be soon. It is your function to hold it to your heart, and offer it to all the world to keep it safe.[415]

UNITY

The following quotes demonstrate God does not judge us. God always sees us as perfect. Nor does God send us to a place called hell. Rather, it is a purification process based on our own righteous judgment. It is not a single event but a continuing process.

> Jesus Christ sees as God sees. He sees the perfection of people;[416]

The great judgment day of Scripture indicates a time of separation between the true and the false. There is no warrant for the belief that God sends man to everlasting punishment. Modern interpreters of the Scripture say that the "hell of fire" referred to by Jesus means simply a state in which purification is taking place.[417]

The "great day of judgment"--which has been located at some fateful time in the future when we all shall be called before the judge of the world and have punishment meted out to us for our sins—is every day.[418]

When we awaken to the reality of our being, the light begins to break upon us from within and we know the truth; this is the quickening of our James or judgment faculty. When this quickening occurs, we find ourselves discriminating between the good and the evil. We no longer accept the race standards or the teachings of the worldly wise, but we "judge righteous judgment"; we know with an inner intuition, and we judge men and events from a new viewpoint.[419]

CHAPTER 9
Healing Consciousness, Establishing Wholeness

―⚬―

WILLINGNESS

WILLINGNESS IS AN IMPORTANT STARTING point for forgiveness in both *A Course in Miracles* and Unity. Willingness represents our openness to question any belief. It lays the groundwork for forgiveness. At the simplest of levels, this willingness is openness to correcting a mistake or error. When we have this willingness, we freely set aside our judgments, decisions, and all we have told ourselves about a person or situation in our lives. In so doing, we let go of our egos/personalities and sense consciousness and open to Christ Consciousness. We are then open to the Truth.

A Course in Miracles

The following quotes demonstrate the importance of willingness in starting the process of moving toward wholeness. This willingness opens us to hearing Truth.

> Healing is a sign that you want to make whole. And this willingness opens your ears to the Voice of the Holy Spirit, Whose message is wholeness. He will enable you to go far beyond the healing

you would undertake, for beside your small willingness to make whole He will lay His Own complete Will and make you whole.[420]

To know reality must involve the willingness to judge unreality for what it is. [421]

The holy instant is the result of your determination to be holy. It is the answer. The desire and the willingness to let it come precede its coming. You prepare your mind for it only to the extent of recognizing that you want it above all else. It is not necessary that you do more; indeed it is necessary that you realize you cannot do more.[422]

The holy instant does not come from your little willingness alone. It is always the result of your small willingness combined with the unlimited power of God's Will.[423]

Unity

In the Unity writings, Charles Fillmore makes a similar assertion about willingness. Here are a few examples:

> One who is housed in the intellect through desire may be ushered into the realm of Spirit by zeal. The first step is a willingness to let go of every thought that holds the ego on the plane of sense.[424]

> In totality John the Baptist represents the perfected natural man who recognizes his finality and his willingness to surrender his personality so that the superman Christ may supplant him, thus symbolizing the evolution of the soul from the personal to the spiritual. [425]

> Sin is the result of desire manifesting itself in erroneous ways. When the error is discovered and there is a willingness to correct it, under the law of forgiveness man erases it easily.[426]

Forgiveness and Repentance

Unity and *A Course in Miracles* offer a very similar meaning of forgiveness. In these teachings, forgiveness releases all mistaken beliefs, resentments, and truly brings about healing.

Unforgiveness is pervasive in our daily lives and throughout the world we see. Unforgiveness is based on judging others. People walk around feeling like victims of each other, the world. When we believe or perceive someone has done something against us or "bad" to us, we hold it against them. They have erred; they are "sinful." We believe they are undeserving of love and deserve punishment of some kind. This is what *A Course in Miracles* calls an attack thought. Punishment can range from simply holding it against them (being unforgiving), to some actual punishment. Even after punishment is rendered, a person can continue to remain unforgiving. This demonstrates that punishment does not lead to the forgiveness we are seeking.

It is important to note we can also judge and attack ourselves with our own thoughts. We hold these judgments against ourselves. We have erred; we are "sinful." We believe we are underserving of love and expect punishment. No matter how much we punish ourselves we continue judging ourselves. As long as we continue judging and attacking ourselves, we cannot experience forgiveness.

Forgiveness releases an ego-based belief that brought about the need for a correction in thinking. In this kind of forgiveness we redirect our thinking away from our ego-based thoughts about life and the world, and then open our minds to direct our thinking toward our True Divinity; it results in a transformation of our perception of the world and each other. Truly used, an act of forgiveness redirects our perception towards seeing the eternal Holiness that is our Divine Nature, both individual and collective. This is why Jesus emphasized the need to forgive.

The central point is that forgiveness is about the change of one's own thoughts which brings about healing of the mind and a state of higher consciousness. This leads to a change in perception of whatever the matter is. Forgiveness is about giving up our error thoughts that are based on human perception which is reliant on the senses and/or cultural traditions in exchange for a perception based on our Higher Nature.

A COURSE IN MIRACLES

Forgiveness is the giving up of an error belief. It is releasing your mind from the wrong perception that another has sinned against you and deserves punishment, or that you have sinned and deserve punishment.

This is a correction in an individual's mind. It is the giving up of a belief that has locked the individual into a limited perception of his/herself, others, or the world. Essentially, forgiveness is the denial of an error judgment; it is recognizing its' falsity, and letting it go.

> What is sin, except a false idea about God's Son? Forgiveness merely sees its falsity, and therefore lets it go. What then is free to take its place is now the Will of God.[427]

> This [the release of the judgment of a brother] is the shift that true perception brings: What was projected out is seen within, and there forgiveness lets it disappear. [428]

> Forgiveness recognizes what you thought your brother did to you has not occurred. It does not pardon sin [error thinking] and make them real. It sees there was no sin. And in that view are all your sins forgiven. What is sin, except a false idea of God's Son? Forgiveness merely sees its falsity, and therefore lets it go. What then is free to take its place is now the Will of God. [429]

> Open your eyes today and look upon a happy world of safety and of peace. Forgiveness is the means by which it comes to take the place of hell. In quietness it rises up to greet your open eyes and

fill your heart with deep tranquility as ancient truths, forever newly-born, arise in your awareness. What you will remember then can never be described. Yet your forgiveness offers it to you. [430]

Unity

Forgiveness is essentially the giving up of the false, erroneous perceptions of the personality/ego for a higher perception. It is about erasing error from the mind while opening to a higher perception or the operation of a higher law.

Charles Fillmore's views on forgiveness also include repentance. However, once again, repentance is not defined in the traditional manner. For Fillmore, forgiveness concerns itself more with a specific error thought, or sin and corresponding event; while repentance is more global, being about the release of our belief in sin or error, and our beliefs in the ways of the world. Repentance is the determination to re-direct our thought system away from these error beliefs to higher thoughts, thoughts in alignment "with" Divine Mind.

> Forgiveness really means the giving up of something. When you forgive yourself, you cease doing the thing that you ought not to do. Man has power to forgive sin [error]. Sin is a falling short of the divine law. Repentance and forgiveness are the only means that man has of getting out of sin [error] and its effect and coming into harmony with the law. All sin is first in the mind; the forgiveness is a change of mind or repentance. We forgive sin [error] in our self every time we resolve to think and act according to the divine law. The mind must change from a material to a spiritual base. Change must all be on the part of man and within him. The moment man changes his thoughts of sickness to thoughts of health the divine law rushes in and begins the healing work. [431]

Forgiveness--A process of giving up the false for the true; erasing sin and error from the mind and body. It is closely related to repentance, which is a turning from belief in sin to belief in God and righteousness. A sin is forgiven when one ceases to sin, and true forgiveness is only established through renewing the mind and body with thoughts and words of Truth....

It is through forgiveness that true spiritual healing is accomplished. Forgiveness removes the errors of the mind, and bodily harmony results in consonance with divine law. [432]

Repentance is a reversal of mind and heart in the direction of the All-Good. When we repent, we break with human thought and ascend into a spiritual thought realm, the kingdom of God.[433]

Miracles

For most people, a miracle is "an extraordinary event manifesting divine intervention in human affairs."[434] Traditional Christianity embraces this definition in relation to the miracles of Jesus which ranged from changing water into wine, healing the sick, to raising the dead. When the term, "miracle," is found in Unity writings it refers to the miracles found in the Bible or something similar. When the term "miracle" is found in *A Course in Miracles*, it does not refer to the extraordinary events found in the Bible.

Even though they use the term miracles differently, both Unity and *A Course in Miracles* are speaking about a shift in consciousness.

When the term, "miracle," is found in Unity writings it refers to the miracles found in the Bible or something similar. While Unity recognizes that these events occurred, "miracles" are NOT seen as divine intervention or an incident that is contrary to or resulting from the suspension of the laws of nature. "Miracles" are seen as the outworking of higher spiritual laws not yet commonly understood by humankind.

In the light of modern science, the miracles of the Bible can be rationally explained as Mind acting in an omnipresent spiritual field, which is open to all men who develop spiritually.[435]

In fact, Charles Fillmore stated that there were no miracles.

There are no miracles in science. Jesus did no miracles. All His marvelous works were done under laws that we may learn and use as He did.[436]

In Unity, a miracle results from the functioning of higher spiritual laws we poorly understand. We learn to understand these higher laws by shifting consciousness to a higher state. Even so, the miracle is still about the seemingly extraordinary events in the physical realm.

In *A Course in Miracles*, the term, "miracle," is used distinctly from the common definition of a miracle. It is NOT a reference to extraordinary events in the physical realm caused by divine intervention or the suspension of natural law. *A Course in Miracles* is NOT about learning how to perform miracles like those reported in the Christian Scriptures. It is about learning how to shift the erroneous, ego driven perceptions of the world towards One-Mindedness.

A miracle is a correction introduced into false thinking by me [Jesus]. It acts as a catalyst, breaking up erroneous perception and reorganizing it properly.[437]

The miracles referred to in *A Course in Miracles* are also about a higher law of truth but NOT about an outer extraordinary event.

And thus it [a miracle] illustrates the law of truth the world does not obey, because it [our worldly view] fails to understand its [miracle] ways.[438]

Essentially, what *A Course in Miracles* calls a miracle is what Unity calls forgiveness. Forgiveness is the giving up of the false, erroneous perceptions of the ego/personality resulting in a shift to a higher level of consciousness.

A COURSE IN MIRACLES

In *A Course in Miracles*, a miracle is the realization of Christ Consciousness and its associated shift to a higher perception, thereby seeing the world differently. This results in the operation of higher law. It is our willingness to see differently that allows the realization of Christ Consciousness which is the miracle. This results in seeing from a higher level of consciousness resulting in the forgiveness of the error perception. In truth, when we see from this higher level of consciousness, realized by the miracle, there is no error in our perception.

When this healing of the mind occurs, the physical body may also be healed. The miracle heals the mind by simply emphasizing Christ Consciousness; any subsequent healing of the body is a physical manifestation of the healed mind. The so-called "healing miracles" of Jesus are the manifestation of Jesus' healed mind accepted, through faith, by the one who was healed.

> The miracle sets reality where it belongs. Reality belongs only to spirit, and the miracle acknowledges only truth. It thus dispels illusions about yourself, and puts you in communion with yourself [your Higher Self] and God. The miracle joins in the Atonement by placing the mind in the service of the Holy Spirit. [439]

> A miracle is a correction.... It merely looks on devastation, and reminds the mind that what it sees is false. It undoes error, but does not attempt to go beyond perception, nor exceed the function of forgiveness... Yet it paves the way for the return of timelessness and love's gentle awakening, for fear must slip away under the gentle remedy it brings.[440]

How just are miracles! For they bestow an equal gift of full deliverance from guilt upon your brother and yourself. Your healing saves him pain as well as you, and you are healed because you wished him well. This is the law the miracle obeys; that healing sees no specialness at all.[441]

Yet must all healing come about because the mind is recognized as not within the body, and its innocence is quite apart from it, and where all healing is. Where, then is healing? Only where its cause is given its effects. ...

...And where effects are gone, there is no cause. Thus is the body healed by miracles because they show the mind made sickness, and employed the body to be victim, or effect, of what it made.[442]

And thus it illustrates the law of truth the world does not obey, because if fails entirely to understand its ways. [443]

UNITY

As stated in the introduction to this section, when the term, "miracle," is found in Unity writings it refers to the "extraordinary events" found in the Bible or something similar. While Unity recognizes that these events occurred, "miracles" are NOT seen as divine intervention or an incident that is contrary to or resulting from the suspension of the laws of nature. Charles Fillmore did not believe miracles occurred as traditionally defined. "Miracles" are seen as the outworking of higher spiritual laws not yet commonly understood by humankind.

In reality miracles are events that take place as a result of the application of a higher law to certain conditions. God never performs miracles, if by miracle is meant a departure from universal law. Whatever the prophets did was done by the operation of laws inherent in Being and open to the discovery of every man.[444]

> The universe was not created through illogical assumptions of law. Law is its foundation. There are no miracles in science. Jesus did no miracles. All His marvelous works were done under laws that we may learn and use as He did. As the body is moved by mind, so the mind is moved by ideas; and right here in the mind we find the secret of the universe.[445]
>
> All true action is governed by law. Nothing just happens. There are no miracles. There is no such thing as luck. Nothing comes by chance. All happenings are the result of cause and can be explained under the law of cause and effect.[446]

When we learn to understand these higher laws by shifting consciousness to a higher state, we, too, can perform "miracles" just like Jesus. Even so, the miracle is still about the seemingly extraordinary events in the physical realm.

> These happenings that seem miraculous are controlled by laws that we have not yet learned and result from causes that we have not been able to understand. Man does not demonstrate according to the law but according to his knowledge of the law, and that is why we must seek to learn more of it. God is law and God is changeless[447]
>
> When men evolve spiritually to a certain degree, they open up inner faculties that connect them with cosmic Mind, and attain results that are sometimes so startling that they seem to be miracle workers. What seems miraculous is the action of forces on planes of consciousness not previously understood. When a man releases the powers of his soul, he does marvels in the sight of the material-minded, but he has not departed from the law. He is merely functioning in a consciousness that has been sporadically manifested by great men in all ages.[448]

Since Unity and *A Course in Miracles* use the term "miracle" differently, is there a term found in Unity that is essentially the same concept as found in the Course? Yes! In this same chapter the topic of forgiveness is reviewed. Unity's definition of forgiveness pretty much makes "forgiveness" a synonym for the way *A Course in Miracles* uses the term, "miracle." Forgiveness is the giving up of the false, erroneous perceptions of the personality/ego for a higher perception. It is about erasing error from the mind by shifting to a higher perception - operation of a higher law.

> Forgiveness really means the giving up of a belief, and any corresponding action or sin. The result is a clearing of our mind, enabling higher thoughts of divine law. [449]

Conclusion (Miracles)

Do we find Unity and *A Course in Miracles* speaking of a shift in consciousness that is the true miracle in a similar manner? Is that shift in consciousness but an "awareness of the operation of a higher law?" Both speak of forgiveness of error thought. Both speak of a higher state of consciousness in which this is realized. Both are focusing on a change in consciousness as the truth of what has been realized.

Whatever words are used to describe the occurrence, we are speaking of the true healing that is the basis for all healing in both of these teachings.

DENIALS AND AFFIRMATIONS

The use of denials and affirmations are found in Unity as well as *A Course in Miracles*. In Unity, denials and affirmations are essential consciousness changers. In *A Course in Miracles* there is a very thorough description of denials and affirmations that is consistent with Unity's teachings. In the *Workbook of A Course in Miracles* each lesson is initiated with a denial or affirmation along the lines of Unity's method.

A Course in Miracles

From the Text, we learn about denials.

> True denial is a powerful protective device. You can and should deny any belief that error can hurt you. This kind of denial is not a concealment [as in contemporary psychology] but a correction. ...In the service of the right mind the denial of error frees the mind, and re-establishes the freedom of the will. When the will is really free it cannot miscreate, because it recognizes only truth.[450]

While focusing on the use of denials to release error thought, the last two sentences speak to the open minded state wherein affirmations, or deeply known Truths, are realized and claimed.

Here is a quote about the appropriate use of denial:

> ... That is why the Bible speaks of "the peace of God which passeth understanding." This peace is totally incapable of being shaken by errors of any kind. It denies the ability of anything not of God to affect you. This is the proper use of denial. It is not used to hide anything, but to correct error. [451]

Here is an example of how *A Course in Miracles* uses denials and affirmations together.

> Fear and love are the only emotions of which you are capable. One [fear] is false, for it was made out of denial; and denial depends on the belief in what is denied [love] for its own existence. By interpreting fear correctly as a positive affirmation of the underlying belief [love] it [fear] masks, you are undermining its [fears] perceived usefulness by rendering it useless. Defenses that do not

work at all are automatically discarded. If you raise what fear conceals [love] to clear-cut unequivocal predominance, fear becomes meaningless. You have denied its [fears] power to conceal love, which was its only purpose.[452]

Much like how Unity defines and uses denials and affirmations, each lesson in *A Course in Miracles Workbook for Students* is stated as one or the other. We are asked to either deny a mistaken belief, or affirm a Truth in each lesson. Examples would include:

I could see peace [Affirmation] instead of this [Denial]. [453]

I am as God created me. [Affirmation] [454]

My part is essential to God's plan for salvation. [Affirmation] [455]

The world I see holds nothing that I want. [Denial] [456]

I loose the world from all I thought it was. [Denial] [457]

I am at home [affirmation]. Fear is a stranger here. [Denial][458]

I bless the world because I bless myself. [Affirmation].[459]

I am in danger nowhere in the world. [A denial-based Affirmation].[460]

UNITY

As described in Unity, denials and affirmations are a means of consciousness changing so that we may realize the Truth, a Higher Consciousness in and of ourselves.

Denial (Unity)

What man forms that is evil they must unform before he can take the coveted step up the mountain of the ideal. Here enters the factor that dissolves the structures that are no longer useful; this factor in metaphysics is known as denial. Denial is not, strictly speaking, an attribute of Being as principle, but it is simply the absence of the impulse that constructs and sustains.[461]

Affirmation (Unity)

> The affirmation is not to make a thing true, but to prepare in consciousness the way of releasing what is already an eternal reality in the superconsciousness. [462]

> To affirm anything is to assert positively that it is so, even in the face of all contrary evidence. We may not be able to see how, by our simply affirming a thing to be true, a thing that to all human reasoning or sight does not seem to be true at all, that we can bring this thing to pass; but we can compel ourselves to cease all futile quibbling and go to work to prove the rule, each one in his or her own life. [463]

> One who knows Principle has a certain inner security given him or her by the understanding of God Mind. Our affirmations are for the purpose of establishing in our consciousness a broad understanding of the principles on which all life and existence depend. [464]

Denials and Affirmations are used together (Unity)

> It is found that, by the use of these mind forces, humanity can dissolve things by denying their existence, and that humanity can build them up by affirming their presence. This is a simple statement,

but when it is applied in all the intricate thought forms of the universe it becomes complex. The law of mental denial and affirmation will prove its truth to all those who persistently make use of it. [465]

Atonement

There is both the process of atonement and the end goal which is the Atonement. Most simply put, the process of atonement is the return to the awareness of Oneness, "oneness with God." The Atonement is accomplished through a continuing practice of forgiveness, returning consciousness to the level of Christ consciousness. Once the Atonement is complete any illusion of separation ends. In Oneness, the Atonement is a state in which there is only God, the totality of Reality.

A Course in Miracles believes the Atonement is both individual and collective. The responsibility lies with each individual and involves total forgiveness by everyone ("every separated Son"); Unity speaks of the atonement as an individual process.

Both teachings agree that the atonement is NOT "the reconciliation of God and man through the sacrificial death of Jesus Christ," nor the "reparation for an offense or injury," (Merriam Webster's on-line dictionary-http://www.merriam-webster.com/dictionary/atonement). Jesus still plays a significant role in the atonement but his role has nothing to do with his crucifixion as a sacrifice. Both *A Course in Miracles* and Unity believe Jesus is the one who recognized the need for atonement and shows us the way.

A Course in Miracles

A Course in Miracles states the return to the awareness of Oneness comes through the Holy Spirit's plan to undo the ego and heal the belief in separation. The Holy Spirit is simply that part of the mind that is still awake to Oneness. The process and the achievement of atonement is our purpose.

This is our journey to awakening to Oneness. The Atonement is completed when all of the Son of God has fulfilled the atonement.

> Atonement - The Holy Spirit's plan of correction is to undo the ego and heal the belief in separation; it came into being with the creation of the Holy Spirit after the separation, and will be completed when every separated Son has fulfilled his part in the Atonement by total forgiveness. [466]

Jesus is in charge of the process of atonement because he began it.

> I am in charge of the process of Atonement, which I undertook to begin.[467]

> There is nothing about me that you cannot attain. I have nothing that does not come from God. The difference between us now is that I have nothing else. This leaves me in a state which is only potential in you.[468]

The Atonement is everybody's responsibility; we are to forgive and correct any belief that blocks us from the Knowledge of God. For nothing else exists. The Manual for Teachers addresses this:

> The sole responsibility of God's teacher [any person who joins the atonement] is to accept the Atonement for himself. Atonement means the correction, the undoing of errors. When this has been accomplished, the teacher of God becomes a miracle worker by definition. [469]

While each one of us is responsible for our Atonement, it is not fully accomplished until it is accomplished by all:

> ...conflict [errors] cannot ultimately be resolved until all the parts of the Sonship have returned [to Oneness]. Only then can

the meaning of wholeness in the true sense be understood. Any part of the Sonship can believe in error or incompleteness if he so chooses. However, if he does so, he is believing in the existence of nothingness. The correction of this error is the Atonement. [470]

Unity

Atonement is when we realize our mind is One with God commonly known as the realization of Oneness. Unity publications span decades. The earliest writings align with the idea that we are responsible for our own atonement while writings published in the 1950s point to Jesus as a kind of intermediary. Currently, "normative Unity" is more in alignment with the earliest published writings. Jesus is the person who shows the way to the atonement. We are to do as he did.

> In our journey back to the Father's house we became lost in our own thought emanations, and Jesus Christ broke through the crystallized thought strata and opened the way for all those who follow him.
>
> By so doing He made a connection between our state of consciousness and the more interior one of the Father—He united them—made them a unit—one, hence at-one-ment or atonement through Him. He became the way by which all who accept Him may "pass over" to the new consciousness. [471]

The way to do this [experience unitive consciousness] is the way Jesus did it. He acknowledged Himself to be the Son of God. The attainment of the Christ consciousness calls for nothing less on our part than a definite recognition of ourselves as sons of God right here and now, regardless of appearances to the contrary." [472]

God is All-Intelligence; there is but the one Mind and in reality there are no separate men and women. [473]

CHAPTER 10

Concepts of the World and the Universe

—w—

Dream / Illusion

A Course in Miracles often refers to the relative realm (the realm of change) as a dream or an illusion. A similar view can be found in Unity writings.

A Course in Miracles

The Course views our separation-based lives and the world we believe in as a projection of our thoughts. It is these projections we perceive as real; these perceptions are but a dream, and illusion. The Absolute Realm or Knowledge of God is our Reality. The Course asserts that nothing outside of our mind actually exists. Just as we make an unreal world in our night-time dreams, the world we see after we seem to wake up has no existence but in our minds.

> The world you see is an illusion of a world. God did not create it, for what He creates must be eternal as Himself. Yet there is nothing in the world you see that will endure forever. ...
>
> For everything they [the bodies eyes] see will not only not last, but lends itself to thoughts of sin and guilt. While everything that God created is forever without sin and therefore is forever without guilt. [474]

Projection makes perception. The world you see is what you gave it, nothing more than that. But though it is no more than that, it is not less. Therefore to you it is important. It is the witness to your state of mind, the outside picture of an inward condition. As a man thinketh, so does he perceive. [475]

Refusing to change your mind will not prove that the separation has not occurred. The dreamer who doubts the reality of his dream while he is still dreaming is not really healing his split mind. You dream of a separated ego and believe in a world that rests upon it. This is very real to you. [476]

And thus will you learn of Him [The Holy Spirit] how to replace your dream of separation with the fact of unity. For the separation [dream] is only the denial of union, and correctly interpreted, attests to your eternal knowledge that union is true. [477]

There is nothing outside you. That is what you must ultimately learn, for it is the realization that the Kingdom of Heaven is restored to you. [478]

A person who identifies with the ego "always perceives this world as outside himself, for this is crucial to his adjustment. He does not realize that he makes this world, for there is no world outside of him. [479]

Dreams show you that you have the power to make a world as you would have it be, and that because you want it you see it. And while you see it you do not doubt that it is real. Yet here is a world, clearly within your mind, that seems to be outside. ... You seem to waken, and the dream is gone. ... And what you seem to waken to is but another form of this same world you see in dreams. All your time is spent in dreaming. Your sleeping and your waking dreams have different forms, and that is all. [480]

Unity

Decades earlier, Charles Fillmore mentions the same concept as found in *A Course in Miracles*: Adam went to sleep, never woke up, and is in a dreamlike state of consciousness. There are additional quotes referencing the dream state.

> A limited concept [dream] of Jehovah God caused a deep sleep (mesmeric state) to fall on the man (Adam). Nowhere in Scripture is there any record to show that Adam was ever fully awakened; and he (man) is still partly in this dreamlike state of consciousness. In this state he creates a world of his own and peoples it with ideas corresponding to his own sleep-benumbed consciousness. [481]

> The sense man is only half-awake, going about in a dream and thinking it is real life. [482]

> He [the separated "son"] is ever in the presence of the Father, and the Father is helping him to awaken from the dream of sense and to judge wisely and to discriminate between the worthwhile things of Spirit and the false and undesirable things of immaturity. [483]

> We are awakening out of our dream and false hope of satisfaction in personal kinship, into the likeness of the God-love in which we feel the joy and the satisfaction of universal brotherhood. [484]

Here are two Unity quote on the world of illusion.

> Spirit is omnipresent, but man has hedged himself about by a world of illusion of his own creating, and through its mists he cannot see the Father, or catch the light from the superconscious mind. [485]

> We must understand clearly that the real life of all men is identical with our own and that aside from the one life all is illusion; [486]

The Physical Universe

A Course in Miracles and Unity teachings agree the physical universe is not a direct creation of God. Both agree that "something happened" in consciousness prior to the appearance of the physical universe.

A Course in Miracles

The seeming existence of the physical is the projection of our mind. We project our thoughts and judgments making up a world based upon our errant belief in separation. What we then perceive in the world is actually a reflection of our thoughts and judgments back to us. Yet, it is our belief in this illusion that perpetuates its seeming existence.

> The world as you perceive it cannot have been created by the Father, for the [real] world is not as you see it. God created only the eternal, and everything you see is perishable. Therefore, there must be another world that you do not see. [487]

> What God did not create does not exist. And everything that does exist exists as He created it. The world you see has nothing to do with reality. It is of your own making, and it does not exist. [488]

> Guilt makes you blind, for while you see one spot of guilt within you, you will not see the light. And by projecting it the world seems dark, and shrouded in your guilt. You throw a dark veil over it, and cannot see it because you cannot look within. [489]

> The gap between reality and dreams lies not between the dreaming of the world and what you dream in secret. They are one. The dreaming of the world is but a part of your own dream you gave away, and saw as if it were the start and ending, both. ...

> You are the dreamer of the world of dreams. No other cause it has, nor ever will. [490]

The "end of the world" further attests to its unreality:

> Can what has no beginning really end? The world will end in an illusion, as it began. Yet will its ending be an illusion of mercy. The illusion of forgiveness, complete, excluding no one, limitless in gentleness, will cover it, hiding all evil, concealing all sin and ending guilt forever. So ends the world that guilt had made, for now it has no purpose and is gone. [491]

UNITY

Many references throughout the Fillmore texts indicate the physical body and the physical universe are not the direct manifestation of God or Divine Mind. The entirety of the relative world is based on Divine Ideas; that does not mean there is a God or Divine Mind intending a physical universe.

> God is not matter nor confined in any way to the idea of substance termed matter. God is that intangible essence which man has "formed" and called matter. Thus matter is a limitation of the divine substance whose vital and inherent character is above all else limitless. [492]

> But God does not form things. God calls from the depths of Its own being the ideas that are already there, and they move forth and clothe themselves with the habiliments [clothes] of time and circumstance in humankind's consciousness. [493]

> The Garden of Eden or Paradise of God is in the ether [Spiritual Substance], and we see that the "fall of man" antedated the formation of this planet as we behold it geologically.

... We are by birth a spiritual race, and we should never have known matter or material conditions if we had followed the leadings of our higher consciousness. [494]

Ages of thought upon the reality and solidity of things have evolved a mental atmosphere that has produced the present material universe. These and millions of other concepts are the work of men [humankind] and not God, as is popularly supposed. However they all rest on the original God-Mind and can be restored to the perfect law and order of that Mind by those who free themselves from the mental entanglements with materiality and identify their thinking with that of the Mind that is Spirit. "Ye shall know the truth, and the truth shall make you free." [495]

The Reason the Physical Universe Happened

As shown above, both agree God did not create the physical world, or matter. Both teachings emphasize it is our seeming separated consciousness, not God, that made the illusory physical world. Each also stresses we have continued to perpetuate belief in the world through our thoughts. So, what happened that caused the physical world? Here, we'll find a slight distinction between the two teachings. In *A Course in Miracles*, the illusory world springs from a thought of separation that is taken seriously; Unity teachings indicate we simply got lost in our own thought creation prior to there even being a physical universe. Both result in a state of guilt.

A Course in Miracles

Into eternity, where all is one, there crept a tiny, mad idea in which the Son of God remembered not to laugh. In his forgetting did the thought become a serious idea, and possible of both accomplishment and real effects. ...

...The world you see depicts exactly what you thought you did.[496]

You who believe that God is fear made but one substitution. It has taken many forms, because it was the substitution of illusion for truth; of fragmentation for wholeness. It has become so splintered and subdivided and divided again, over and over, that it is now almost impossible to perceive it once was one, and still is what it is. That one error, which brought truth to illusion, infinity to time, and life to death, was all you ever made. Your whole world rests upon it. ...

You may be surprised to hear how very different is reality from what you see. You do not realize the magnitude of that one error. It was so vast and so completely incredible that from it a world of total unreality had to emerge. What else could come of it? Its fragmented aspects are fearful enough, as you begin to look at them. But nothing you have seen begins to show you the enormity of the original error, which seemed to cast you out of Heaven, to shatter knowledge into meaningless bits of disunited perceptions, and to force you to make further substitutions. ...

That was the first projection of error outward. The world arose to hide it, and became the screen on which it was projected and drawn between you and the truth. [497]

The acceptance of guilt into the mind of God's Son was the beginning of the separation, as the acceptance of the Atonement is its end. The world you see is the delusional system of those made mad by guilt. Look carefully at this world, and you will realize this is so. For this world is the symbol of punishment, and all the laws that seem to govern it are the laws of death. [498]

The world is nothing in itself. Your mind must give it meaning. And what you behold upon it are your wishes, acted out so you can look on them and think them real. Perhaps you think you did not make the world, but came unwillingly to what was made already, hardly waiting for your thoughts to give it meaning. Yet in truth you found exactly what you looked for when you came.

There is no world apart from what you wish, and herein lies your ultimate release. [499]

As a reminder, the separated son of God is dreaming the illusory, physical universe into existence. In a fearful state, one can envision the need to attempt to resolve the fear with a seeming solution; the ego's seeming solution is the world. This is why The Course states, "The world was made as an attack on God."

The world was made as an attack on God. It symbolizes fear. And what is fear except loves absence? Thus the world was meant to be a place where God could enter not, and where His Son could be apart from Him. Here was perception born … [500]

UNITY

According to Charles Fillmore:

The Ideas of God are potential forces waiting to be set in motion through proper formative vehicles. The thinking faculty of man is such a vehicle, and it is through this that the visible universe has existence. [501]

In this [dreamlike] state [of consciousness] he [man] creates a world of his own and peoples it with ideas corresponding to his own sleep-benumbed consciousness. [502]

You could not have been made by this infinite Mind and been perfect without your cooperation. You are an identity in yourself. How did you attain that identity of yourself? By expressing

> the potentialities of Being. In other words, you took your share of substance from the Father Mind, and took it away, in a measure. You separated yourself from that substance, and if you carry that to the excess of the part of race consciousness, you develop a sense of separation such that you forget all about the Source; consequently, you are in a state of guilt. If you are not perpetually, drawing from the Father Mind, you will find eventually there will be a famine in your country. You will have a lack of vigor, vitality, energy, and life. [503]

The implication is our thoughts make the world we see; they are thoughts of separation and not of Oneness. Ultimately, separation consciousness always leads to lack and a world based on fear beliefs and guilt.

> When it [consciousness] looks wholly without, upon sensation and feeling, it loses its bearings in the maze of its own thought creations. Then it builds up a belief of separateness from, and independence of, a causing power. Man sees only form, and makes his God a personal being located in a city of dimensions. This belief of separateness leads to ignorance, because all intelligence is derived from the one Divine Mind, and when the soul thinks itself something alone, it cuts itself off in consciousness from the fount of inspiration. Believing himself separate from his source, man loses sight of the divine harmony. [504]

> The I AM has its being in heaven; its home is in the realm of perfect ideals, the Christ within, but it has its freedom. It loves to be. To be is to enjoy. To enjoy is for the time to be that which we enjoy. When you are absorbed in the recital of an interesting story, you are lost to all else. The I AM is for the moment identified with that which it enjoys. Here is the solution of a great mystery--how the I AM ever came to separate itself from its sphere of wisdom.
> But it is wonderfully simple when you understand it. You are demonstrating the so-called fall of man every time you lose

yourself in the whirl of sense pleasure. The mission of the I AM is happiness. It seeks joy and bliss; they are set before it in unstinted measure, and it revels in their intoxicating draughts, but the mastery of the higher mind should ever be maintained. [505]

Time

Both teachings point to the unreality of time. Time is a construct of human consciousness. And yet, we can use our belief in time in a constructive way.

A Course in Miracles

The world of time is an illusion. [506]

No man cometh unto the Father but by me" does not mean that I am in any way separate or different from you except in time, and time does not really exist.[507]

Ultimately, space is as meaningless as time. Both are merely beliefs. [508]

The Atonement *principle* was in effect long before the Atonement began. The principle was love and the Atonement was an act of love. Acts were not necessary before the separation, because belief in space and time did not exist.[509]

Each day, and every minute in each day, and every instant that each minute holds, you but relive the single instant when the time of terror took the place of love. And so you die each day to live again, until you cross the gap between the past and present, which is not a gap at all. Such is each life; a seeming interval from birth to death and on to life again, a repetition of an instant gone by long ago that cannot be relived. And all of time is but the mad belief that what is over is still here and now. [510]

Even though time is not real, we can still use it in productive ways.

The purpose of time is to enable you to learn how to use time constructively. It is thus a teaching device and a means to an end. Time will cease when it is no longer useful in facilitating learning. [511]

Now you must learn that only infinite patience produces immediate effects. This is the way in which time is exchanged for eternity. Infinite patience calls upon infinite love, and by producing results now it renders time unnecessary. We have repeatedly said that time is a learning device to be abolished when it is no longer useful. The Holy Spirit, Who speaks for God in time, also knows that time is meaningless. [512]

Unity

Time is of the physical, relative world. It is as much a construct of human consciousness as is space.

The consciousness that we have fulfilled the divine law in both thought and act is the Sabbath. It has nothing to do with any day of the week. God did not make days and weeks, nor has He darkened His clear concepts of Truth by the element of time. Time is an invention of the human. [513]

Time is a human invention and acts as a barrier to a broader conception of creative processes. All attempts to find a date for the beginning of man are futile. Years are associated with events, and when the events are past the years go with them. States of mind make events, and new states of mind are constantly being formed; consequently every moment is the beginning of a new creation to the individual. It is of no practical value to a man to know that the world has journeyed around the sun six thousand or six million years since it was formed. The important thing is to know where man stands in relation to the creative law. [514]

Even though time is a human invention, we can still make good use of it. Time is the measure that man gives to passing events. The only power in time is what imparts to it. When man gets into the understanding of the Absolute, he takes his freedom from all bondage of time and declares that time shall no more enter into the substance of his mind or body or affairs.[515]

The "Real World"

A Course in Miracles

There is a reference to a "real world" as well. Again like the world referred to above, the "real world" exists only as a function of our projection and perception; it, too, is an illusion. The difference is the "real world" is perceived from the highest level of consciousness, referred to as true perception. The real world is comprised of our real thoughts, those thoughts that are loving, and therefore eternal. When this is known, an instant later, the "real world" is no longer, for the Atonement is complete, and all that is is God.

> There is a borderland of thought that stands between this world and heaven. It is not a place, and when you reach it is apart from time. …
>
> This is the journey's end. We have referred to it as the real world. And yet there is a contradiction here, in that the words

imply a limited reality, a partial truth, a segment of the universe made true. This is because knowledge makes no attack upon perception. They are brought together, and only one continues past the gate where Oneness is. [516]

Every loving thought that the Son of God ever had is eternal. The loving thoughts his mind perceives in this world are the world's only reality. They are still perceptions, because he still believes that he is separate. Yet they are eternal, because they are loving. ... The real world can actually be perceived. All that is necessary is a willingness to perceive nothing else.

Perceiving only the real world will lead you to the real Heaven, because it will make you capable of understanding it. [517]

UNITY

Three references to the "real world" can be found in a few of the published Unity books. In addition to these references, it is important to point out that the term, "Spiritual Universe," is nearly a synonym for the term, "real world," found in *A Course in Miracles*.

God-Mind presents its perfect ideals to all minds, especially to those that are open to the light of the Christ, by whom the bonds of error thought are broken. Those who have been trained to think of God as a person, as the parent of a family of billions can continue to think of Him as such by adding the attributes of unlimited principle. But they should not make their God a man with the limitations of the human. The natural man thinks that the world in which he lives is the real world and that the thoughts he thinks are the real thoughts. [518]

Apparently we live in two worlds: an invisible world of thoughts, and a visible world of things. The invisible world of thought substance is the real world, because it is the source of the world of things, and man stands between the two, handing out with his thoughts the unlimited substance of Spirit. When man gets understanding of the right relation between the visible and the invisible into his mind and active in his thought, all his needs will be met. That is what Jesus meant when He said, "Seek ye first his kingdom, and his righteousness; and all these things shall be added unto you." [519]

And when we are thoroughly translated into the knowledge that "the lower world is made after the pattern of the upper and inner world," then will we have power over all these appearances of sense.

> This inner world is the subjective, the real world, the intelligible world. [520]

In the six mental steps or "mind movements," called days, Elohim God creates the spiritual universe and spiritual man. He then rests. He has created the ideas or patterns of the formed universe to follow. [521]

Heaven and the Universe

References in *A Course in Miracles* and in Unity point to the existence of the universe in a different manner, different from our conventional thought of a "physical" universe. Both teachings point to the existence of a Universe that is God; it is speaking of the "Heavens" or the Spiritual Universe as our True Reality, as Spirit.

A Course in Miracles

Consider the following quotes to learn *A Course in Miracles'* concept of the Universe. As you read them notice that the use of the term "universe" is a reference to the Absolute Realm of Knowledge that is God and not to the physical universe.

> Turn to the Name of God for your release, and it is given you…
> All little things are silent. Little sounds are soundless now. The little things of earth have disappeared. The universe consists of nothing but the Son of God, who calls upon his Father. [522]

> There are no beginnings or endings in God, Whose universe is Himself. Can you exclude yourself from the universe, or from God Who is the universe? …
> The laws of the universe do not permit contradiction. What holds for God holds for you. If you believe you are absent from God, you will believe that He is absent from you. Infinity is meaningless without you, and you are meaningless without God. There is no end to God and His Son, for we *are* the universe. [523]

> …the Kingdom of Heaven is restored to you. For God created only this and He did not depart from it nor leave it separate from Himself. The Kingdom of Heaven is the dwelling place of the son of God, who left not his Father and dwells not apart from him. Heaven is not a place or a condition. It is merely an awareness of perfect oneness, and the knowledge that there is nothing else; nothing outside this oneness, and nothing else within. [524]

Unity

While Unity uses the term "universe" to refer to the physical universe, there are instances where the term "universe" is used in a similar way to

A Course in Miracles. The Universe is God, or Divine Mind, and is sometimes called the Spiritual Universe or Heaven.

> The material universe is only the out picturing of the spiritual universe. [525]

> In the six mental steps or "mind movements," called days, Elohim God creates the spiritual universe and spiritual man. He then rests. He has created the ideas or patterns of the formed universe that is to follow. [526]

> God ideated two universal planes of consciousness, "the heavens and the earth." One is the realm of pure ideas, the other of thought forms. God does not create the visible universe directly, as a man makes a concrete pavement, but He creates the ideas that are used by His intelligent "image and likeness" to make the universe. Thus God's creations are always spiritual. Man's creations are both material and spiritual, according to his understanding. [527]

CHAPTER 11

The Physical Body, Sickness and Healing

THE BODY AND THE PHYSICAL universe are not creations of God. Both teachings view the physical universe and the physical body as projections of our consciousness based on our belief in separation. The physical universe and physical bodies are viewed as illusions; matter is not real therefore the physical body is not real. God created us as only Spirit, our True Reality.

The body seems so real to us that it is difficult to think of ourselves as anything more than a mind encased within a body. Many also think of themselves as a body having a mind. This close identification with the body can make it difficult to realize we are more than a body and simply *seem* to have a body.

Both teachings agree that the body is not our true nature. We are Spirit. Even so, the teachings treat the body somewhat differently. In the Unity writings, there is evidence that the healing of the physical body is a goal in and of itself. But in *A Course in Miracles*, the body can be no more than a tool of the mind to achieve true perception (a state where we are ready to know only Oneness).

Unity speaks of the development of the body utilizing the terms degeneration, and generation. Degeneration equates to what *A Course in Miracles* refers to as the fall in consciousness. This fall in consciousness is expressed through a belief in the existence of the body. Degeneration refers to both the original fall in consciousness as well as any ongoing beliefs, thoughts, feelings and actions that result in a belief in the physical universe and the physical body.

Generation is the Unity term for procreation. There is no corresponding discussion about procreation or sexuality in *A Course in Miracles* as originally published by the Foundation for Inner Peace, the most commonly known version. It is important that we acknowledge that there is information on sexuality in the more recently published Urtext edition. This version is not within the scope of this book. (See "How to use this book.")

A Course in Miracles

The Body

God/Divine Mind has no part in the existence of the physical body. The body is a projection of the mind immersed in separation consciousness. As such, the body is used to demonstrate separation is real and that we are apart from one another and God. As a result, the need to maintain the body's existence becomes a predominate focus.

> God did not make the body, because it is destructible, and therefore not of the Kingdom. The body is the symbol of what you think you are. It is clearly a separation device, and therefore does not exist. [528]

> The body is the instrument the mind made in its efforts to deceive itself. Its purpose is to strive. [529]

> The body is a tiny fence around a little part of a glorious and complete idea. It draws a circle, infinitely small, around a very little segment of Heaven, splintered from the whole, proclaiming that within it is your kingdom, where God can enter not. [530]

> The body is outside you, and but seems to surround you, shutting you off from others and keeping you apart from them, and them from you. It is not there. There is no barrier between God and His Son, nor can His Son be separated from Himself except

in illusions. This is not his reality, though he believes it is. . You cannot put a barrier around yourself, because God placed none between himself and you. [531]

The Course realizes the notion that bodies do not really exist is difficult to swallow, and it expects the reader to have a negative reaction to the idea. It specifically advises us *not* to attempt to deny the body's existence.

There is a wariness that is aroused by learning that the body is not real. [532]

It is almost impossible to deny its existence in this world. Those who do so are engaging in a particularly unworthy form of denial. [533]

The Source of Sickness
Sickness perpetuates the belief in separation. The following quotes speak to the source of bodily sickness:

If you let your mind harbor attack thoughts, yield to judgment or make plans against uncertainties to come, you have again misplaced yourself, and made a bodily identity which will attack the body, for the mind is sick. [534]

The ego has a profound investment in sickness. If you are sick, how can you object to the ego's firm belief that you are not invulnerable? This is an appealing argument from the ego's point of view, because it obscures the obvious attack that underlies the sickness. If you recognized this and also decided against attack, you could not give this false witness to the ego's stand. [535]

The body can appear to change with time, with sickness or with health, and with events that seem to alter it. Yet this but means the mind remains unchanged in its belief of what the purpose of the body is.

Sickness is a demand the body be a thing that it is not. Its nothingness is guarantee that it can *not* be sick. In your demand that it be more than this lies the idea of sickness. [536]

Sickness is anger taken out upon the body, so that it will suffer pain. [537]

A sick and suffering you but represents your brother's guilt; the witness that you send lest he forget the injuries he gave, from which you swear he never will escape. [538]

The Body as a Tool of the Mind
The Course speaks of the body as simply a tool of the mind, a communication device of consciousness based on separation. Its purpose is determined by one's individual consciousness. From separated consciousness, the body is used for attack and is prone to sickness and aging. Under the Holy Spirit's guidance, the body can be used for communicating with others, as a means for salvation and for purposes of love instead of fear. The Course even implies that when the mind is completely healed, the body will become immune to sickness, and free from any limitation imposed by time, weather, fatigue, food, or drink.

> The body appears to be largely self-motivated and independent, yet it actually responds only to the intentions of the mind. If the mind wants to use it for attack in any form, it becomes prey to sickness, age and decay. If the mind accepts the Holy Spirit's purpose for it instead, it becomes a useful way of communicating with others, invulnerable as long as it is needed, and to be gently laid by when its usefulness is over. Of itself it is neutral, as is everything in the world of perception. [539]

Would you not have the instruments of separation [bodies] reinterpreted as means for salvation, and used for purposes of love? ... Your perception of the body can clearly be sick, but project not this upon the body. [540]

Remember that the Holy Spirit interprets the body only as a means of communication. ... The ego separates through the body. The Holy Spirit reaches through it to others. [541]

Perhaps you do not realize that this removes the limits you had placed upon the body by the purposes you gave to it. As these are laid aside, the strength the body has will always be enough to serve all truly useful purposes. The body's health is fully guaranteed, because it is not limited by time, by weather or fatigue, by food and drink, or any laws you made it serve before. You need do nothing now to make it well, for sickness has become impossible. [542]

The Healing Process

Prior to healing, the body is a learning device used to perpetuate the belief in separation. Since the mind is the source of the body, the mind is the only place true healing can occur. Through changed perception, healing of the physical occurs such that the body becomes a useful tool in the Son of God's communication process. It is important to emphasize that the changing of consciousness and perception is the goal. Healing of the body is simply an effect of that goal.

Healing is the result of using the body solely for communication. [543]

Every situation, properly perceived, becomes an opportunity to heal the Son of God. And he is healed because you offered faith to him giving him to the Holy Spirit and releasing him from every demand your ego would make of him. ...The body is healed because you came without it, and joined the Mind in which all healing rests.

The body cannot heal, because it cannot make itself sick. It needs no healing. Its health or sickness depends entirely on how the mind perceives it, and the purpose the mind would use it for. It is obvious that a segment of the mind can see itself as separated from the Universal Purpose. When this occurs the body becomes its weapon, used against this Purpose, to demonstrate the "fact" that separation has occurred. The body thus becomes an instrument of illusion ...[544]

Yet must all healing come about because the mind is recognized as not within the body, and its innocence is quite apart from it, and where all healing is. Where, then is healing? Only where its cause is given its effects. ...

And where effects are gone, there is no cause. Thus is the body healed by miracles because they show the mind made sickness, and employed the body to be victim, or effect, of what it made. [545]

Defend the body and you have attacked your mind. For you have seen in it the faults, the weaknesses, the limits and the lacks from which you think the body must be saved. You will not see the mind as separate from bodily conditions. And you will impose upon the body all the pain that comes from the conceptions of the mind as limited and fragile, and apart from other mind and separate from its Source.

These are the thoughts in need of healing, and the body will respond with health when they have been corrected and replaced with truth. This is the body's only real defense. Yet is this where you look for its defense? [546]

The body needs no healing. But the mind that thinks it is a body is sick indeed![547]

The lesson is the *mind* was sick that thought the body could be sick... [548]

Here is a Workbook lesson of the healing experience as it specifically relates to the mind and is subsequently realized through a transformed perception of the body:

Sickness is a defense against the truth. I will accept the truth of what I am, and let my mind be wholly healed today.
    Healing will flash across your open mind, as peace and truth arise to take the place of war and vain imaginings. ... It [your mind] will be healed of all the sickly wishes that it tried to authorize the body to obey.
    Now is the body healed, because the source of sickness has been opened to relief. And you will recognize you practiced well by this: The body should not feel at all. ... Its usefulness remains and nothing more.
    Perhaps you do not realize that this removes the limits you had placed upon the body by the purposes you gave to it. As these are laid aside, the strength the body has will always be enough to serve all truly useful purposes. The body's health is fully guaranteed, because it is not limited by time, by weather, or fatigue, by food or drink, or any laws you made it serve before. You need do nothing now to make it well, for sickness has become impossible. [549]

UNITY

The Body
Consistent with his views on the world, Charles Fillmore stated that the physical body is "the outer expression of consciousness; the precipitation of the thinking part of man." God is not directly manifesting or creating the physical body. There are 3 terms found in Unity literature that are

related to concepts about the body. They are degeneration, generation, and regeneration. These topics are included below.

> Body – The outer expression of consciousness; the precipitation of the thinking part of man. God created the idea of the body of man as a self-perpetuating, self-renewing organism, which man reconstructs into his personal body. God creates the body idea, or divine idea, and man, by his thinking, makes it manifest.[550]

Degeneration

The physical body comes about through a fall in consciousness that Charles Fillmore calls degeneration.

> When the Adamic race reached a point in their evolution where they had personal-will volition, they began to think and act independently of the Jehovah or Christ Mind. Then the sense consciousness began to rule and the materialization of the body resulted. Degeneration of the whole man followed. Loss of ability to draw constantly on the one and only source of life threw the whole race into an anemic condition. Their bodies began to disintegrate, and death came into the world. Then Satan, the mind of sense, began to rule; sin was in the saddle. The people like sheep had gone astray; they were lost in the wilderness of sense; they were in the throes of race extinction. [551]

> When the soul of the race became involved in the pleasures of sensation and sought other guidance than that of Jehovah God, gradual degeneration of the whole human family began until men were in a bad way. Something had to be done. Someway, somehow we had to be lifted out of the murky darkness of sense thought. Jesus Christ provided and provides today the greatest impetus to the ongoing of our race. [552]

The Source of Sickness

Similar to *A Course in Miracles*, the source of sickness is in the mind. It is caused by a negative attitude, sin (missing the mark, error), "ungodlike thought," as well as laws of sickness formed by the human race that reside in race (collective) consciousness.

> ... a negative attitude brings its train of sin, sickness, poverty, and death. [553]

> body, effects of sin and righteousness on the--The body is destroyed, made sick unto death by sin and ignorance; ....[554]

> Man seeking happiness through sense pleasure. This is sin (missing the mark), and the wages are pain, sickness, poverty, and death. [555]

> Mortal mind breeds sin, poverty, sickness, and death. [556]

> race consciousness--The human race has formed laws of physical birth and death, laws of sickness and physical inability, laws making food the source of bodily existence, laws of mind that recognize no other source of existence except the physical. The sum total of these laws forms a race consciousness separate from and independent of creative Mind. [557]

Generation

> generation--Procreation. The law of generation is undoubtedly the mystery of mysteries in human consciousness. Men have probed, with more or less success, all the secrets of nature, but of the origin of life they know comparatively nothing. It is only when the inquiring mind transcends the human and rises into the spiritual realm that light comes. [558]

The idea that man is the product of physical generation is an error of race ignorance. Man's understanding that he is in reality brought forth through the action of the mind will restore him to the divine law under which he will increase, multiply, and replenish the earth according to the plan of God's creation. [559]

So, when man loses his body by death, the law of expression works within him for re-embodiment, and he takes advantage of the Adam method of generation to regain a body. [560]

The Healing Process

Healing comes about by changing the mind as found in *A Course in Miracles*. There is a subtle and important difference. In *A Course in Miracles*, changing the mind is the goal while the healed body is the effect of the changed mind. Again, in Unity, it is more like the healed body is the goal and changing the mind is the means for achieving it.

> Consciousness must harmonize with God-Mind to be free from thoughts of poverty, sin, sickness, and death. [561]

> Through the Christ Mind we find salvation from poverty, sickness, sin, and death. [562]

> All healing is based on mental cleansing. When the mind is free from error thoughts, harmony in the body ensues. Permanent healing is never accomplished until the mental cause of the disease, the error thought, is removed. [563]

> It is through forgiveness that true spiritual healing is accomplished. Forgiveness removes the errors of the mind, and bodily harmony results in consonance with divine law. [564]

While Unity does not speak of a better use of the body as found in *A Course in Miracles*, it does speak to what happens when the body is manifested from "conscious union with Divine Mind." When this happens the body manifests perfection.

> Body, redemption of -- The body is made and sustained by thought. Its character is like the thought that made it. Every thought has in it an idea of substance and life. When the mind of man is in conscious union with Divine Mind his body manifests perfection. [565]

Threefold Nature: Spirit-Soul-Body

In both, we find a teaching about the threefold nature of humankind which is Spirt-soul-body. Where:

- Spirit is our Divine Nature; it is Absolute.
- Soul is mind; it is relative.
- Body is the physical body; it is relative.

In *A Course in Miracles* we can find references to Spirt, mind and body. A distinction between the two does occur around the emphasis placed on the body.

A Course in Miracles

In *A Course in Miracles* we find that Spirit is already illuminated and not requiring any correction. The mind serves as the creative expression of Spirit. However, the mind can and does mis-create through the belief in separation. A major demonstration of the belief in separation is the body. The mind then mis-perceives itself within a body. Once the mind mis-perceives itself within the body, the way back to wholeness is through using the body, under the guidance of Spirit, as a learning device to heal and correct the mind.

> Only the mind can create because spirit has already been created, and the body is a learning device for the mind. [566]

> Spirit makes use of mind as means to find its Self expression. And the mind which serves the spirit is at peace and filled with joy. Its power comes from spirit, and it is fulfilling happily its function here. Yet mind can also see itself divorced from spirit, and perceive itself within a body it confuses with itself. Without its function then it has no peace, and happiness is alien to its thoughts. [567]

> To amplify an earlier statement, spirit is already perfect and therefore does not require correction. The body does not exist except as a learning device for the mind. This learning device is not subject to errors of its own, because it cannot create. [568]

> Only the mind is capable of illumination. Spirit is already illuminated and the body in itself is too dense. The mind, however, can bring its illumination to the body by recognizing that it is not the learner, and is therefore unamenable to learning. The body is, however, easily brought into alignment with a mind that has learned to look beyond it toward the light. [569]

UNITY

In Unity, the threefold nature of humankind is seen as a whole. Spirt, soul (mind) and body are three aspects of the same thing. This is still in the context of the physical universe and the body being an illusion as discussed in Chapter 10.

Man is spirit, soul, body. These are coexistent. God is the principle of being as an axiom is a principle of mathematics. God is not confined to locality. Is a mathematical principle confined to a particular place and not found elsewhere? "The kingdom of God is within you." God is the real of man's being. It follows that all the powers that are attributed to God may become operative in man. ...

Man sets into action any of the three realms of his being, spirit, soul, and body, by concentrating his thought on them. If he thinks only of the body, the physical senses encompass all his existence. If mind and emotion are cultivated he adds soul to his consciousness. If he rises to the Absolute and comprehends Spirit, he rounds out the God-man. [570]

Spirit

Spirit in you is you. You are Spirit. It is the whole of you which you may be expressing in part. [571]

In its higher functioning the mind of humankind deals with spiritual ideas, and we can truthfully say that everyone is a spiritual being. [572]

Soul

Charles Fillmore frequently used the term soul to mean the relative mind, the sum total of the conscious and subconscious minds. Other times, he used it in the traditional sense where Soul means Spirit or Divine Mind.

Soul - Humankind's consciousness; the underlying idea back of any expression. In humankind, the soul is the many accumulated ideas back of his or her present expression. In its original and true sense, the soul of each person is the expressed idea of humankind in Divine Mind ... soul includes the conscious and subconscious minds. [573]

Soul unfoldment means the bringing forth of divine ideas in the soul or consciousness of humankind and the bringing of these ideas into expression in the body. [574]

Body

Body – the outer expression of consciousness; the precipitation of the thinking part of man. God created the idea of the body of man as a self- perpetuating, self-renewing organism, which man reconstructs into his personal body. God creates the body idea, or divine idea, and man, by this thinking, makes it manifest. [575]

The body of a person is the visible record of his or her thoughts. [576]

CHAPTER 12

Unity's Twelve Powers

—⚏—

UNITY FEATURES A UNIQUE RANGE of material on developing Christ Consciousness, which revolves around the teaching on the Twelve Powers, with related material on degeneration and regeneration.

As we have said, *A Course in Miracles* is more focused on undoing of the ego belief system, while Unity's focus is about developing Christ Consciousness. In this chapter the material is only from Unity writings. The only topics in this chapter that have related material in *A Course in Miracles* are Christ and Christ Consciousness, which are covered in Chapter 3 of this book in the section on "Son of God, Sonship, Christ."

CHRIST

UNITY

In the Absolute, the unchanging Realm of Reality, there is Christ, an Idea made up of Ideas. It is an Idea/Ideal to be expressed. Other names for the Christ are the I Am, the Word, Son of God, Superconsciousness. This Christ is the Truth of each and every person.

> In every person the Christ, or Word of God, is infolded; it is an idea that contains ideas. [577]

The second in the Trinity is the Son. ...The Son of God is the fullness of the perfect-man idea in Divine Mind. ... The Son ever exists in God. Father and Son are one and are omnipresent in the universe. [578]

This brings us to the true estimate of man, and when we speak of spiritual man, or Christ man, or the son of God, we refer to this original expression of Divine Mind. [579]

Christ Consciousness

Unity

Christ Consciousness is expressed or made manifest from the Idea or Principle called Christ. Christ Consciousness is much like True Perception found in *A Course in Miracles* (refer to the section "the ego," found in Chapter 5). It is a consciousness from which each person can see and perceive only Itself, Christ Consciousness. It is sometimes referred to as the regenerated state. Christ Consciousness is sometimes called Superconsciousness or Christ Mind.

> We are joint heirs with Christ to all that the Father has. This truth alone--the belief that in the regenerate state we are to be like Jesus, who became Christ manifested--leads us to a desire and an effort to attain our inheritance of eternal life here and now, because we know that there is no other thing in the universe worth striving for. [580]

> SUPERCONSCIOUSNESS is the goal toward which humanity is working. Regardless of appearances there is an upward trend continually active throughout all creation. ...

...The superconsciousness has been perceived by the spiritually wise in every age, but they have not known how to externalize it and make it an abiding state of consciousness. Jesus accomplished this, and His method is worthy of our adoption, because as far as we know, it is the only method that has been successful....

... Jesus acknowledged Himself to be the Son of God. Living in the superconsciousness calls for nothing less on our part than a definite recognition of ourselves as sons of God right here and now, regardless of appearances to the contrary. We know that we are sons of God; then why not acknowledge it and proceed to take possession of our God heirdom?[581]

Developing Christ Consciousness – General

Unity

Christ Consciousness is achieved by clearing up the erroneous ego thoughts/feelings.

> In the journey from sense to Spirit the soul passes through many phases, misdirects its faculties, and practices multitudinous forms of dissipation or waste. ... But as man follows the light as it is given him to see the light, he gradually learns to understand himself and his soul activities. Then he begins to conform to spiritual law and to conserve his energies, forces, and substance, which in turn results in lifting up the whole man, spirit, soul, and body, out of the mire of materiality and sense into the new estate of the regenerate man, the Jesus Christ man. [582]

> Christian metaphysicians have discovered that man can greatly accelerate the growth in himself of the Christ Mind by using affirmations that identify him with the Christ. These affirmations

often are so far beyond the present attainment of the novice as to seem ridiculous, but when it is understood that the statements are grouped about an ideal to be attained, they seem fair and reasonable. [583]

Step by step, thought added to thought, spiritual emotion added to spiritual emotion--eventually the transformation is complete. It does not come in a day, but every high impulse, every pure thought, every upward desire adds to the exaltation and gradual personification of the divine in man and to the transformation of the human. The "old man" [the ego or personality] is constantly brought into subjection, and his deeds forever put off, as the "new man" appears arrayed in the vestments of divine consciousness. [584]

In *A Course in Miracles*, the process of undoing the ego is through practicing the lessons of the workbook.

Regeneration

Unity

Christ Consciousness is achieved through regeneration, a conscious effort to elevate sense consciousness. Regeneration is explained in general terms as well as in the context of the Twelve Powers.

Regeneration is the term Charles Fillmore used for the process of realizing the Christ Potential. Regenerating the mind would then reflect in the physical body. There is more on this process in Chapter 11, The Physical Body, Sickness and Healing. The need for regeneration arises from degeneration.

Degeneration refers to both the "original fall" in consciousness as well as any ongoing beliefs, thoughts, feelings and actions that result in a fall in consciousness. Degeneration in consciousness leads to beliefs in separation which gives rise to the physical universe and the physical body.

> When once the ideal man is conceived in the mind as a possibility, and the requirements of the Law are complied with, the regeneration of mind and body is under way; then he who descended is no longer hampered by the thought of sinful flesh; he is glorified with the manifestation of divine substance in his body. [585]

> regeneration--A change in which abundant spiritual life, even eternal life, is incorporated into the body. The transformation that takes place through bringing all the forces of mind and body to the support of the Christ ideal. The unification of Spirit, soul, and body in spiritual oneness.
> Regeneration begins its work in the conscious mind and completes it in the subconsciousness. The first step is cleansing or denial in which all error thoughts are renounced. This includes [our] forgiveness for sins committed and a general clearing of the whole consciousness. After the way has been prepared, the second step takes place.
> This is the outpouring of the Holy Spirit. [586]

Regeneration is neither a theory nor a fad; it is a spiritual ideal. It is not an opinion to be held, but a life to be lived. It is a spiritual quickening which purifies, refines and exalts the soul [conscious and subconscious mind], and it gradually brings the mind and body under the dominion of the Christ Mind. It is a process of unfoldment. The culmination of this growth in the Jesus Christ consciousness expressed as a resurrected life. Because regeneration is both a principle and the practice of the principle, it should not be confused with anybody's idea of what it might be, nor with anybody's opinion of what it should be. The real knowledge of it comes through the Holy Spirit of Truth in your own heart. Follow it always, and you will be led into Truth and nothing but the Truth. [587]

Regeneration and the Twelve Powers

Unity

The Twelve Powers are a means of developing Christ Consciousness and are referenced in one way or another in many of the writings of Charles and Myrtle Fillmore. The Powers are called by various names: Faculties, Divine Ideas and Abilities. As a reminder, there is no direct parallel of this concept in *A Course in Miracles*, although The Course does present a similar notion of gradual reclamation of our true spiritual nature. But it does not try to identify the many characteristics of this Identity, in the way that Unity does.

Unity speaks of the Christ as being an Idea made up of multiple Ideas. It is made up of the Twelve Divine Ideas, which are the Twelve Powers. They are: Faith, Strength, Judgment, Love, Power, Wisdom, Imagination, Understanding, Will, Order, Zeal, Elimination and Life. Since each of us is this Christ Idea in potential, each of us has these powers. We have them whether or not we know it. Our job is to become aware of them and then to begin consciously using them. The goal is to use them in their highest capacity. This process realizes Christ Consciousness from the Christ Idea. However, when we use them from the ego, sense level, we often get unwanted results.

> When Jesus had attained a certain soul development, He called His twelve apostles to Him. This means that when man is developing out of mere personal consciousness into spiritual

consciousness, he begins to train deeper and larger powers; he sends his thought down into the inner centers of his organism, and through his word quickens them to life. Where before his powers have worked in the personal, now they begin to expand and work in the universal. [588]

Definitions of each of the Twelve Powers based on Charles Fillmore's book, The Twelve Powers of Man and other writings:

<u>Faith</u> – The ability to believe, intuit, perceive, to have conviction, and to "hear."
<u>Strength</u> – The ability to endure, stay the course, last, be persistent, persevere, and to be stable.
<u>Judgment/Wisdom</u> – The ability to judge, evaluate, discern, be wise, appraise, to know how to use what you know, and to apply what you know.
<u>Love</u> – The ability to desire, harmonize, unify, attract oneself to, and to feel affection for.
<u>Power/Dominion</u> – The ability to master, dominate, and control.
<u>Imagination</u> – The ability to image, picture, conceptualize, envision, and dream.
<u>Understanding</u> – The ability to know, perceive, comprehend and apprehend.
<u>Will</u> – The ability to choose, decide, command, lead, and determine.
<u>Order/ Spiritual Law</u> – The ability to organize, balance, sequence, and adjust.
<u>Zeal</u> – The ability to be enthusiastic, be passionate, start, motivate, and be impulsive.
<u>Elimination/Renunciation</u> – The ability to release, remove, denounce, deny, and let go.
<u>Life</u> – The ability to energize, vitalize, enliven, animate and invigorate.[589]

How to Develop the Twelve Powers

The Twelve Powers are developed by "calling them out." We claim them through the Power of the Word in the form of affirmations.

Unity

In the regeneration we release these powers. You are all in the regeneration if you are awakening the spiritual man, if you really have faith in this Christ I AM within you to call out these powers, or these faculties[590]

THE SUBCONSCIOUS realm in man has twelve great centers of action, with twelve presiding egos or identities. ... when man is developing out of mere personal consciousness into spiritual consciousness, he begins to train deeper and larger powers; he sends his thought [affirmations] down into the inner centers of his organism, and through his word quickens them to life. Where before his powers have worked in the personal, now they begin to expand and work in the universal. This is the first and the second coming of Christ, spoken of in the Scriptures. The first coming is the receiving of Truth into the conscious mind, and the Second Coming is the awakening and the regeneration of the subconscious mind through the superconscious or Christ Mind. [591]

Here are affirmation for each of the Powers.

Faith:
I claim Faith now. I believe and except I am Christ.

Strength
I claim Strength now. Regardless of the circumstances, I stay the course so I can live from my Christ Potential.

Wisdom
I claim Wisdom now. I use Wisdom to compare and contrast my thoughts, ideas, beliefs and images so I am living from my Christ Potential.

Love
I claim Love now. I use Love to deeply desire to know the Christ Potential I already am.

Dominion
I claim Dominion now. I use Dominion to control erroneous thinking while I master living from my Christ Potential.

Imagination
I claim Imagination now. I visualize and see myself living from my Christ Potential.

Understanding
I claim Understanding now. I know what it takes to live from my Christ Potential.

Will
I claim Will now. I easily choose to live from my Christ Potential in all circumstances.

Order
I claim Order now. I use Order to adjust and balance my thoughts and feelings so I am living from my Christ Potential.

Zeal
I claim Zeal now. I passionately and enthusiastically live from my Christ Potential.

Elimination

I claim Elimination now. I easily renounce any erroneous thoughts and beliefs that hinder my living from my Christ Potential.

Life

I claim Life now. I use Life to energize and vitalize living from my Christ Potential. [592]

Epilogue

WE HAVE COMPARED AND CONTRASTED the teachings of A *Course in Miracles* and those found in various Unity materials. Our intention has been to bring these teachings together and to demonstrate how strikingly similar they are. While there are distinctions, those distinctions can be worked together or one after the other to actually advance and accelerate our spiritual awakening. They are not antagonistic; they are synergistic. This book is not intended to be a substitute for the learning and application of the teachings found in either *A Course in Miracles* or Unity.

The language used to express the Truths is both similar and distinct. Both use traditional Judeo-Christian terminology in redefined ways. Both refer to God as He or Him despite their assertion that God is neither male nor female and is not a being, entity or person. Even so, we have explored some concepts that are the same but the terminology to refer to then differs. One simple example is that the *A Course in Miracles* term, miracles, is pretty much equivalent to the way Unity defines forgiveness – a shift in perception from error to Truth.

The most fundamental and underlying Truth found in both teachings is that God is our one and only Reality. They say we are an Idea in the Mind of God or God-Mind. It is a timeless, unchangeable Reality that can never be lost regardless of mistaken beliefs in separation and duality. Ultimately our journey or process is to undo these mistaken beliefs and to claim to Truth of our Divine Reality.

Both teachings embrace the Judeo-Christian concept of a fall or separation from God as written about in the allegory of Adam and Eve in the Garden of Eden. Somehow, someway this erroneous belief begins in the Son of God and continues to be perpetuated today in humankind. While this seeming separation begins as a mere thought in consciousness it ultimately results in the manifestation of the entire physical universe which includes our individual bodies. Even so, in our timeless, unchanging Absolute Reality this fall has never occurred.

The relative, changing state of reality and the physical universe all begin and are sustained through the erroneous mental perceptions and constructs of our relative belief system in our seemingly separated mind. Separation is based on beliefs in time, space and physicality all rooted in limitation and lack as demonstrated in our limited consciousness and the world around us.

In both teachings, Jesus is not uniquely the Son of God or God as traditionally understood. Jesus is presented as the man who awakened to the infinite Christ Consciousness that is the Truth of everyone. He realized this Divine Reality in himself and saw it in others. He introduced teachings that anyone can use to realize this same potential. Jesus is not the great exception; Jesus is the great example for all of us to follow. He opened the way in consciousness.

One great strength of *A Course in Miracles'* is the workbook, the means by which the ego's erroneous thought system is recognized, neutralized and forgiven. Unity's great strength is found in the teaching of the 12 Powers which are used to upgrade thoughts, ideas, beliefs and images held in consciousness from error to Truth. As said before, these distinctions actually can amplify each other and produce a greater opportunity for expanding spiritual awareness and the realization of Oneness.

Ultimately, both teachings provide a path toward living from a higher state of Consciousness, through relinquishing thoughts of separation while embracing Oneness. What more could we ask? Thank you, Unity and *A Course in Miracles* for lighting our path.

BIBLIOGRAPHY AND RESOURCES

Note: A conscious decision was made to stray from some of the norms of bibliographic citations.

- A few books have no author and are a compilation of quotes from either Charles or Myrtle Fillmore from a variety of publications. These are cited as if they were written by Charles or Myrtle Fillmore.
- United States postal abbreviations for states are utilized.

A Course in Miracles

A Course in Miracles, Combined Volume: Text, Workbook for Students, and Manual for Teachers. 2nd ed. Glen Allen, CA: Foundation for Inner Peace, 1992.

A Course in Miracles, Manual for Teachers. 2nd ed. Glen Allen, CA: Foundation for Inner Peace, 1992.

A Course in Miracles, Text. 2nd ed. Glen Allen, CA: Foundation for Inner Peace, 1992.

A Course in Miracles, Workbook for Students. 2nd ed. Glen Allen, CA: Foundation for Inner Peace, 1992.

The Song of Prayer- Prayer, Forgiveness, Healing - An Extension of the Principles of

A Course in Miracle. 2nd ed. Mill Valley, CA: Foundation for Inner Peace, 1992.

Wapnick, Kenneth, Ph.D., *Glossary-Index for A Course in Miracles*. 4th Edition, Roscoe, NY: Foundation for "A Course in Miracles," 1993.

UNITY

Metaphysical Bible Dictionary. Unity Village, MO: Unity House, 1931.

Butterworth, Eric. *Discover the Power within You: A Guide to the Unexplored Depths Within.* 1968. 40th anniversary ed. New York: HarperOne, 2008.

Butterworth, Eric. *Celebrate Yourself!* Unity Village, MO: Unity Books, 1984

Butterworth, Eric. *You and Your Mind.* Unity Magazine 161, November 1981.

Cady, H. Emilie. *Lessons in Truth.* 1903. Centennial ed. Unity Village, MO: Unity House, 2003.

Fillmore, Charles. *Atom-Smashing Power of Mind.* 1949. 2nd ed. Unity Village, MO: Unity House, 2006.

Fillmore, Charles. *Christian Healing.* 1909. First Unity Classic Library ed. Unity Village, MO: Unity House, 2004.

Fillmore, Charles. *Dynamics for Living: A Topical Compilation of Essential Fillmore Teachings.* Selected and arranged by Warren Meyer. Unity Village, MO: Unity House, 1995.

Fillmore, Charles. "*Extracts from Letters: Regeneration.*" Unity 54:1 (Jan 1921).

Fillmore, Charles. *Jesus Christ Heals.* 1939. 2nd ed. Unity Village, MO: Unity House, 1940.

Charles Fillmore. *Keep a True Lent.* 2nd ed., Unity Village, MO: Unity House, 2005.

Fillmore, Charles. *Mysteries of Genesis*. 1936. 2nd ed. Unity Village, MO: Unity House, 2007.

Fillmore, Charles. *Mysteries of John*. 1946. 2nd ed. Unity Village, MO: Unity House, 2008.

Fillmore, Charles. *Prosperity*. 1936. Unity Village, MO: Unity House, 21st printing.

Fillmore, Charles. *Releasing the Holy Spirit of God in Man*. Unity Village, MO: Unpublished lesson, 1931.

Fillmore, Charles. *Talks on Truth*. 1934. 3rd rev. ed. Unity Village, MO: Unity House, 1989.

Fillmore, Charles. *Two Undisciplined States of Consciousness*. Unity Village, MO: Unpublished Sunday lesson, April 12, 1931.

Fillmore, Charles and Cora Fillmore. *Teach Us to Pray*. 1941. 2nd ed. Unity Village, MO: Unity House, 2007.

Fillmore, Charles. *The Revealing Word: A Dictionary of Metaphysical Terms*. 1959. 2nd ed. Unity Village, MO: Unity House, 2006.

Fillmore, Charles. *The Twelve Powers of Man*. 1930. Unity Village, MO: Unity House, 1999.

Fillmore, Connie. *Keys to the Kingdom: Five Fundamentals of Truth*. Unity Village, Mo.: Unity School of Christianity, 1990.

Fillmore, Myrtle. *How to Let God Help You*. Selected and arranged by Warren Meyer. 1956. 3rd ed. Unity Village, MO: Unity House, 2000.

Fillmore, Myrtle. *Myrtle Fillmore's Healing Letters.* (Also published as *Letters of Myrtle Fillmore.*) Compiled by Frances W. Foulks. 1936. Paperback ed. Unity Village, MO: Unity House, 2006.

Hasselbeck, Paul and Cher Holton. *Power UP: The Twelve Powers Revisited as Accelerated Abilities.* Durham, NC: Prosperity Publishing House, 2010.

Hasselbeck, Paul and Cher Holton, *PowerUP Card Set.* Durham, NC: Prosperity Publishing House, 2009.

Sikking, Sue. *Beyond a Miracle.* Unity Village, MO: Unity School of Christianity, 1973

WEB RESOURCES

Bible Study Tools, http://www.biblestudytools.com/dictionaries/eastons-bible-dictionary/trinity.html

Merriam-Webster, beta, http://www.merriam-webster.com/dictionary

Science and Nonduality, "Nonduality." http://www.scienceandnonduality.com/nondulity.shtml

Authors' Short Biographies

William Heller

Reverend William Heller is an ordained Unity Minister, committed to deepening and sharing his spiritual journey through teaching, writing and spiritual counseling. Bill's formal training was in corporate finance, leading to a 30 year career, primarily in Silicon Valley. Mid-way through, Bill had an awakening experience, which led to a redirection in his life towards spiritual awakening. Within two years of that experience, Bill found the teachings of *A Course in Miracles* and Unity as his path. Fifteen years later, He entered the Unity Institute of Spirituality's ministry program, and was ordained in 2009. He has served in ministry at Unity Churches in New England and Virginia—a marked change from his previous 40 years in California.

Bill shares his life with his wife, Kathleen, and live in Western Connecticut. Together they share their lives with their combined 7 children and 13 grandchildren.

Paul Hasselbeck

Rev. Dr. Paul Hasselbeck, formerly Dean of Spiritual Education and Enrichment for Unity Institute, currently serves as Spiritual Education and Enrichment (SEE) full time faculty. Paul was the Minister of Pastoral Care and Prayer at Unity Church of Overland Park and was a retreat minister for Unity Village Retreats. He is the author of <u>Point of Power</u>, and <u>Heart-centered Metaphysics</u>. He co-authored <u>Applying Heart-Centered Metaphysics</u> and <u>PowerUP</u>, a 12 Powers text and card set, with Rev. Dr. Cher Holton. Paul also co-authored <u>Get Over</u> It and <u>Get Over These</u> with Rev. Dr. Bil Holton. For seven years, Paul hosted Metaphysical Romp, a weekly internet radio program, on Unity.fm. He now co-hosts Metaphysical Romp II with the Rev. Drs. Bil and Cher Holton. It is all about metaphysical theory, supportive science and practical application. These programs are archived for your enjoyment. Paul lives in Overland Park, Kansas, with two Yorkshire Terriers (Mackie and Monet).

ENDNOTES:

Chapter 1: Laying the Groundwork

1. Fillmore, Charles. *Jesus Christ Heals*. 1939. 2nd ed. Unity Village, MO: Unity House, 1940. p. 129
2. *A Course in Miracles, Combined Volume: Text, Workbook for Students, and Manual for Teachers.* 2nd ed. Glen Allen, CA: Foundation for Inner Peace, 1992. Text, 1.I.33:1-4, p. 5
3. Text, 1.I.37; 1-2, p, 5
4. Workbook, P.II.13.2.2, p. 473
5. Fillmore, Connie. *Keys to the Kingdom: Five Fundamentals of Truth*. Unity Village, MO: Unity School of Christianity, 1990. p. 5
6. Fillmore, Charles. *Christian Healing*. 1909. First Unity Classic Library ed. Unity Village, MO: Unity House, 2004. p.10
7. Fillmore, Charles. *Talks on Truth*. 1934. 3rd rev. ed. Unity Village, MO: Unity House, 1989. p.11
8. Text, 7.IV.7:4-5, p. 119
9. Text, 10.IV.4:4, p. 188
10. Workbook, P.1.156.2:5-9, p. 294
11. *Keys to the Kingdom*, p. 5
12. Fillmore, Charles. *Dynamics for Living: A Topical Compilation of Essential Fillmore Teachings*. Selected and arranged by Warren Meyer. Unity Village, MO: Unity Books, 1995. pp. 46-47
13. *Jesus Christ Heals*, p. 157
14. Workbook, P.I.110.8:1, p. 200
15. Workbook, P.I.110.9:4, p. 200
16. Manual, Clarification of Terms, 5.2:1-2; 3:1, p. 87
17. *Keys to the Kingdom*, p. 5
18. Fillmore, Charles, *The Revealing Word: A Dictionary of Metaphysical Terms*. 1959. 2nd ed. Unity Village, MO: Unity House, 2006. p. 193
19. Ibid, p. 155
20. Text, 2.VI.9:14, p. 31
21. Text, 21 Intro.1:1-6, p. 445

22. Text, 5.V.4:1-2, p. 84
23. Text, 7.II.2:4-5, p. 114
24. Workbook, P.II.325.1:1-4, p. 464
25. *Keys to the Kingdom*, p. 5
26. *The Revealing Word*, p. 152
27. Fillmore, Charles. *Atom-Smashing Power of Mind*. 1949. 2nd ed. Unity Village, MO: Unity House, 2006. p. 104
28. Text, 1.I.11:1-3, p. 3
29. Text, 9.II.3:1-2, p. 164
30. *The Song of Prayer: Prayer, Forgiveness, Healing; An Extension of the Principles of A Course in Miracles*. 2nd ed. Mill Valley, CA: Foundation for Inner Peace, 1992. 1.I.1:6 -7, p.1
31. *Keys to the Kingdom*, p. 5
32. *The Revealing Word*, p. 86
33. Workbook, Introduction 1:1-2, p. 1
34. Text, 4.VI.6:2-3, p. 68
35. Text, 11.VIII.5:3, p. 212

Chapter 2: One Presence, One Power What is and What is Not

36. Science and Nonduality, "Nonduality." http://www.scienceandnonduality.com/nonduality.shtml (accessed September 14, 2014)
37. Text, 14.IV.1:7-8, p. 279
38. Text, 29-I.1:1, p. 606
39. Workbook, P.I.83.3:2-3, p. 148
40. Text, 18.VI.1:5-6, p. 384
41. Workbook, P.I.95.12:2, p. 168
42. Text, 3.V.7:1-4, p. 45
43. Text, 7.IV.7:3-6, p. 119
44. Text, Introduction, p. 1
45. Text, 30.VIII.2:9, p. 643
46. Text, 30.VIII.4:1-2, p.643

47. Text, 3.II.3:6, p. 39
48. Fillmore, Myrtle. *How to Let God Help You.* Selected and arranged by Warren Meyer. 1956 3rd ed. Unity Village, MO: Unity House, 2000. p. 25
49. Fillmore, Charles, *Christian Healing*, p.97
50. Fillmore, Charles, *Atom-Smashing Power of Mind*, p. 93
51. Fillmore, Charles, *Talks on Truth*, p. 149
52. Fillmore, Charles, *Christian Healing*, p. 56
53. Wapnick, Kenneth, Ph.D., *Glossary-Index for A Course in Miracles*, 4th ed. Roscoe, NY: Foundation for A Course in Miracles, 1993. p.187
54. Text, 16.V.15:3-4, p. 344
55. Text, 13.VIII.3:5, p. 258
56. Manual for Teachers, 2.2:6-8, p. 5
57. Fillmore, Charles, *Revealing Word*, p. 127
58. Fillmore, Charles, *Atom-Smashing Power of Mind*, p. 93
59. *Christian Healing*, p. 55
60. Fillmore, Charles and Cora Fillmore. *Teach Us to Pray.* 1941. 2nd ed. Unity Village, MO: Unity House, 2007. pp. 130-131
61. Preface, p. x
62. Text, 3.III.2.10, p. 40
63. Text, 3.III.1:5-6, p. 40
64. Preface, p. x
65. Text, 11.VII.1:1-3, p. 210
66. Workbook, P.I.23.4.1-3, p.34
67. *The Revealing Word*, p. 7
68. *Atom- Smashing Power of Mind*, p. 88
69. *The Revealing Word*, p. 163
70. *Atom-Smashing Power of Mind*, p. 88
71. *The Revealing Word*, p. 134
72. Ibid, p. 177
73. Ibid, p. 185
74. Text, 4.III.3.2-5, p. 60
75. Text, 3.IV.2:2-3, p. 42

76. Text, 4.II.4:3-5, 7, p. 57
77. Workbook, P.I.25.2:1-2, p. 38
78. *Christian Healing*, p.58
79. *The Revealing Word*, pp. 148 - 149
80. Ibid, p. 61
81. Text, 7.VI.10:4-6, pp. 125-126
82. Text, 2.VI.9:3-8, p. 31
83. Text, 6.II.8:1-2, 4, p. 97
84. *Atom-Smashing Power of Mind*, pp. 93-94
85. Fillmore, Charles, *Mysteries of Genesis*. 1936. 2nd ed. Unity Village, MO: Unity House, 2007. p. 26
86. *Christian Healing*, p. 6
87. Manual, 12.6:2-11, p. 32
88. Text, 5.III.11:1, p. 80
89. Workbook, P.I.23.2:3-7, p.34
90. Workbook, P.I.132.5:1-2, p. 242
91. Text, 31.VIII.4.1-3, p. 667
92. Text, 31.VIII.6:2-3, 5, p. 667
93. *The Revealing Word*, p. 31
94. Fillmore, Charles. *Mysteries of John*. 1946. 2nd ed. Unity Village, MO: Unity House, 2008. p. 29
95. *The Revealing Word*, p. 8
96. Ibid, p. 195
97. Bible Study Tools, http://www.biblestudytools.com/dictionaries/eastons-bible-dictionary/trinity.html, (accessed July 1, 2015)
98. Text, 3.II.5:4-6, p. 39
99. Text, 8.IV.8:9-12, p. 146
100. Fillmore, Myrtle, *How to Let God Help You*, p. 25
101. Fillmore, Charles, *Christian Healing*, p. 20
102. Text, 4.VII.5:1, p. 70
103. Text, 30.III.4:5-6, 9-10, p. 631
104. Text, 4.VII.6:1-3, pp. 70-71
105. 105 Fillmore, Charles, *Dynamics for Living*, p. 22

106. Cadie, H. Emilie, *Lessons in Truth*. 1903. Unity Village, MO: Unity Books, Unity Classic Library. 1995. p. 18
107. Workbook, P.II.222.1:1, 3, p. 402
108. Text, 2.I.3:9, p. 18
109. Manual for Teachers, 21.5:8-9 p.54
110. *Dynamics for Living*, p. 31
111. *Lessons in Truth*, pp.17-18
112. Fillmore, Charles. *Prosperity*. 1936. Unity Village, MO: Unity House, 21st printing. p. 14
113. Text, 15.VI.4:4, p. 315
114. Manual For Teachers, Clarification of Terms, 1.1:1-2, p. 79
115. Workbook, P.I.45, p. 71
116. Wapnick, Kenneth, Ph.D., *Glossary-Index for A Course in Miracles*. p.150
117. Text, 11.I.6:4-5, p. 195
118. Fillmore, Charles, *Atom-Smashing Power of Mind*, p. 93
119. Fillmore, Charles, *The Revealing Word*, p. 56
120. Ibid, p. 84
121. *Atom-Smashing Power of Mind*, p. 93
122. Fillmore, Charles, *Mysteries of Genesis*, p. 12
123. Fillmore, Charles. *Releasing the Holy Spirit of God in Man*, Lesson 1. 1931. Unpublished pp. 1-3
124. Text, 7.I.7:5-7, p.113
125. Text, 19.IV.D 1:4, p. 420
126. Text, 4.III.1:5, p. 60
127. Text, 2.I.1:2, p. 17.
128. Text, 7.I.5:2, p. 113
129. *How to Let God Help You*, p. 41
130. *Atom-Smashing Power of Mind*, p. 93
131. *Mysteries of Genesis*, p. 14
132. Text, 9.I.9:7, p. 162
133. Text, 10.V.7:6, p. 191
134. Workbook, P.I. Rev.V.4:3 p. 329

135. *Christian Healing*, p. 139, quoting I John 4:8
136. Fillmore, Charles, *Talks on Truth*, p. 52
137. *Myrtle Fillmore's Healing Letters.* (Also published as *Letters of Myrtle Fillmore.*) Compiled by Frances W. Foulks. 1936. Rev. Paperback ed. Unity Village, MO: Unity House, 2006. pp. 112-113
138. Fillmore, Charles, *Jesus Christ Heals*, p. 27
139. Text, 2.VII.3:11, p. 32
140. Text, 9.I.9:6, p. 162
141. Fillmore, Charles. *The Twelve Powers of Man.* 1930. Unity Village, MO: Unity House, 1999. p. 52
142. *The Revealing Word*, p. 32
143. *Dynamics for Living*, p. 28
144. Text, 5.II.1:6-7, p. 75
145. Text, 6.I.19:1, p. 96
146. Text, 10.V.9:9, p. 191
147. Text, 11.III.5:7, pp. 199-200
148. *The Revealing Word*, p. 96
149. *Dynamics for Living*, p. 250
150. Fillmore, Charles, *Mysteries of John*, p. 137
151. Text, 2.II.4:2-3, p. 19
152. Text, 9.I.11:3, p. 162
153. Text, 25.IX.5:4, p. 539
154. Manual, Clarification of Terms, 6.3:1, 4, p. 89
155. *Dynamics for Living*, p. 30
156. Fillmore, Charles, *Christian Healing*, p. 16
157. *The Revealing Word*, p. 72
158. Text, 3.II.5:4-6, p.39
159. Text, 4.IV.10:1, p. 64
160. Text, 28.II.1:1-6, pp. 592-593
161. Manual, Clarification of Terms, 1.1: 3-4, p. 79
162. Text, 1.I.3:4-6, p. 10
163. Text, 3.IV.5:11, p. 43
164. Text, 3.V.7:3-4, p. 45
165. Text, 1.I.19:2, p. 4

166. Text,1.VII.3:14, p. 15
167. Text, 2.VII.6:2-5, p. 33
168. Fillmore, Charles. *Keep a True Lent.* 2nd ed., Unity Village, MO: Unity House, 2005, p. 173
169. Ibid, p. 165
170. *The Revealing Word*, p. 123
171. Butterworth, Eric. *Discover the Power within You: A Guide to the Unexplored Depths Within.* 1968. 40th anniversary ed. New York: HarperOne, 2008. p. 12
172. *The Revealing Word*, p. 181
173. Text, 5.I.4:1-2, p. 73
174. Manual, Clarification of Terms, 6.3:1-3, p.89
175. Manual, Clarification of Terms 6.4:1-10, pp. 89-90
176. Text, 5.III.1:4, p. 78
177. Workbook, P.I.43.1:3-7, p. 67
178. Manual, Clarification of Terms, 6.1:1, p.89
179. Manual, Clarification of Terms, 6.5:1, p. 90
180. Text, 30.II.3:3, p. 629

Chapter 4: Who is Jesus, Who am I?

181. Workbook, P.I.152.12:2, p. 283
182. Fillmore, Myrtle, *How to Let God Help You*, p. 86
183. Fillmore, Charles, *Jesus Christ Heals*, p. 194
184. Fillmore, Charles, *Mysteries of John*, p.19
185. Fillmore, Charles, *Dynamics for Living*, p. 39
186. Manual, Clarification of Terms, 5:2:1-2, 3:1-2, p. 87
187. Text, 4.I.13:5, p. 56
188. Butterworth, Eric, *Discover the Power within you*, p. 20
189. Fillmore, Charles, *The Revealing Word*, pp. 110-111
190. Fillmore, Charles, *Atom Smashing Power of Man*, pp. 40-41
191. Text, 2.I.3:6-8, p. 18
192. Fillmore, Charles, *Mysteries of Genesis*, p. 41

193. Wapnick, Kenneth, Ph.D., *Glossary-Index for A Course in Miracles*, 1993, p. 65
194. Text, 4.II.3:1-2, 4:3-4, pp. 56-57
195. Text, 4.IV.1:1-7, pp. 62-63
196. Workbook, P.I.25.2:2, p. 38
197. Text, 4.V.4:1-3, p. 66
198. Text, 18.VIII.1:6-7, 2:5-6, p. 390
199. Workbook, P.I.199.1:1-4, p. 382
200. *The Revealing Word*, p. 62
201. Ibid, p. 6
202. Ibid, pp. 148-149
203. Cady, H. Emilie, *Lessons in Truth*, pp. 88-89
204. *Atom-Smashing Power of Mind*, pp. 116-117
205. Text, 2.VII.6:1-3, p. 33
206. Text, 6.II.8:1-2, 4-5, p. 97
207. Text, 5.II.10:1, p. 77
208. Text, 3.II.5:1-2, p. 39
209. *Discover the Power Within You*, p. 12
210. *Mysteries of Genesis*, p. 12
211. Fillmore, Charles, *Keep a True Lent*, p. 63
212. *The Revealing Word*, p. 34
213. *Keep a True Lent*, p. 165
214. Fillmore, Charles, *Dynamics for Living*, p. 120
215. Text, Preface, pp. viii-ix
216. Text, 1.II.3:10-13, p. 7
217. *The Revealing Word*, p. 34
218. Fillmore, Myrtle, *Myrtle Fillmore's Healing Letters*, p. 30
219. *Teach Us to Pray*, p. 130

Chapter 5: Separation, Relative Mind and the Ego

220. Text, 8.V.2:8, p. 147
221. Workbook, P.II.6.2:1, p. 431

222. Text, 6.II.10:7, p. 98
223. Text, 27.VIII.6:2-3, pp. 586-587
224. Text, 22.II.9:1-3, p. 473
225. Text, 12.III.9:1, 6, p. 222
226. Text, 2.VII.5:5-7, p. 32
227. Fillmore Charles, *Christian Healing*, p. 66
228. Fillmore, Charles, *Jesus Christ Heals*, p. 37
229. Fillmore, Charles, *Keep a True Lent*, p. 54
230. Fillmore, Charles, *Talks on Truth*, p. 10
231. Fillmore, Charles, *Teach Us to Pray*, p. 160
232. Wapnick, Kenneth, Ph.D., *Glossary-Index for A Course in Miracles*, p. 148
233. Ibid, p. 150
234. Text, 7.VI.9:1-3, p. 125
235. Text, 3.IV.2:1-3; 3.1-6, p. 42
236. Text, 3.IV.5:1-9, pp. 42-43
237. *Manual for Teachers, Clarification of Terms*, 1.5:2; 6:1-2, p. 79
238. Text 3.IV.4:1, 3, p. 42
239. Text, 3.IV.2:3, p. 42
240. Text 4.II.10:1-2, p. 59
241. Fillmore, Charles, *The Revealing Word*, p. 133
242. Ibid, p. 134
243. Ibid, p. 134
244. Ibid, p. 133
245. Ibid, p. 134
246. Ibid, p. 84
247. Ibid, p. 142
248. *Glossary-Index for A Course in Miracles*, p.7
249. Text, 4.VI.1:6, p. 67
250. Text, 4.VII.1.5, p. 69
251. Workbook, P.II.12.1:1, p. 467
252. Text, 3.IV.2:2-3 p.42
253. Workbook, P.I.25.2:2, p. 38
254. *Glossary-Index for A Course in Miracles*, 4th ed., p. 65

255. Ibid, p. 65
256. Ibid, p. 228
257. Ibid, p. 178
258. Text, 3.IV.4:3-4, p. 42
259. Workbook, P.I.96.4:1-5, p. 169
260. Workbook, P.I.151.4:2-5, p. 278
261. Text, 4.II 4.3-4, 7-8, 10-11; 7:8-9, pp. 57-58
262. Text, 7.VIII.4:7-8, 5:1-2, 6:1, 7:1-5, p. 131
263. *The Revealing Word*, p. 61
264. Ibid, p. 61
265. Fillmore, Charles, *Mysteries of Genesis*, pp. 137-138
266. *Christian Healing*, p. 59

Chapter 6: Specialness

267. Text, 1.V.3:5-8, pp. 12-13
268. Text, 15.V.10:5-6, p. 314
269. Fillmore, Charles, *Talks on Truth*, p. 143
270. Fillmore, Charles, *Keep a True Lent*, p.32
271. Ibid, p. 169
272. *Talks on Truth*, pp. 94-95
273. Text, 24.III.7:1-6, p. 507
274. Text, 20.VI.8:6-8, p. 438
275. Text, 20.VI.11:1-3, p. 438
276. Text, 20.VII.5:1-4, p. 440
277. *Talks on Truth*, pp. 163-164
278. Text, 24.II.1:1-2, p.502
279. Text, 24.VI.11:1-3, p. 513
280. Text, 24.IV.1:1-4, p. 507
281. Text, 24.4:2, 4-5, p. 500
282. Fillmore, Charles, *Christian Healing*, p. 122
283. Text, 16.V.1:1-4, p. 341
284. Text, 16.V.9:3, p. 343

285. Text, 24.II.2:1, 7, p. 502
286. Text, 15.V.2:2-6, p. 312
287. Text, 15.V.4:1-4, p. 312
288. Fillmore, Charles, *Mysteries of John*, p. 17
289. *Christian Healing*, p. 125
290. Fillmore, Charles. *Two Undisciplined States of Consciousness.* Unity Village, MO. Unpublished Sunday lesson, April 12, 1931. pp. 12-13
291. Text,,16.V.4:3
292. Text, 24.I.3:1-2, 5-6, p. 500
293. Text, 24.I.9:1-2, p. 501
294. Text, 24.VII.1:1, 3, 6, p. 514
295. *Metaphysical Bible Dictionary.* Unity Village, Missouri: Unity House, 1931. p. 576
296. Text, 16.IV.8:4, p. 399
297. Text, 17.IV.2:3-4, p. 358
298. Text, 17.V.2:1-2, p. 362
299. Text, 16.V.4:1-4, p. 341
300. Text, 20.VI.8:3-4, pp. 437-438
301. Text, 16.VI.4:4, p. 345
302. Text, 16.V.12:2-4, p. 343
303. Text, 15.V.6:1-5, p. 313
304. Text, 24.I.4:2-7, p. 500
305. Text, 22.Intro.2:5-8, 3:1-6, p. 467
306. Text, 15.V.4:5-6, 5:1-3. pp. 312-313
307. Text, 16.IV.1:1-3, p. 337
308. Text, 17.III.3:1-2, 4, p. 355
309. Text, 20.VI.8:3-8, pp. 437-438
310. Text, 15.V.3:3, 5-6 p. 312
311. Text, 15.V.8:1-4, p. 342
312. Text, 16.VI.1:1-4, p. 345
313. Text, 16.IV.7:1-2, pp. 338-339
314. Text, 16.V.3:1, 3-5, 8, p. 341
315. Text, 17.III.4:1, 3-8, p. 355
316. Text, 16.IV.1:3, 5-6, p. 337

317. Text, 16.IV.3:1-2, 4-7, pp. 337-338
318. *Talks on Truth*, p. 81
319. Fillmore, Charles, *Dynamics for Living*, p. 121
320. Fillmore, Charles, *Jesus Christ Heals*, p. 62
321. Fillmore, Myrtle, *Healing Letters*, pp. 144-145
322. Ibid, pp. 147-148
323. *Talks on Truth*, p. 151

Chapter 7: The Holy Instant, the Holy Relationship

324. Text, 15.V.1:1-2, p. 312
325. Text, 15.V.9:1-7, pp. 313-314
326. Text, 15.V.10:8-10, p. 314
327. Text, 15.V.8: 2, p. 313
328. Text, 17.V.1: 1, 6-7, p. 362
329. Fillmore, Myrtle, *Myrtle Fillmore's Healing Letters*, p. 105
330. Fillmore, Charles, *Keep a True Lent*, p. 32
331. Fillmore, Charles, *The Revealing Word*, p. 182
332. Workbook, P.I.69 title, p. 117
333. Text, 25.I.6:1, p. 520
334. Text, 25.VI.4.1-2, p. 530
335. Text, 25.VI.7:1-4, p. 530
336. Text, 25.VI.7:6-8, p. 530
337. Text, 25.VI.6:6-8, p. 530
338. Fillmore, Charles, *Atom-Smashing Power of Mind*, pp. 38-39
339. Fillmore, Charles, *Christian Healing*, p. 126
340. *Christian Healing*, pp. 125-126
341. Text, 17.V.1.1, p. 362
342. Text, 17.V.2, p. 362
343. Text, 15.VIII.3:8, p. 321
344. Text, 13.X.11:1-2, p. 265
345. Text, 24.I.6:1-2; 7:1-3, 5-6, p. 501
346. Text, 20.V.5:1-4, p. 435

347. Cady, H. Emilie, *Lessons in Truth*, p. 150
348. *Keep a True Lent*, pp. 56-57
349. *Christian Healing*, p. 120
350. Ibid, p.120
351. *Keep a True Lent*, p. 95
352. Text, 1.V.3:5-6, p. 12
353. Text, 22.in.1:7, p. 467
354. Text, 17.V.2:2, 4, 3:9, p. 362
355. Text, 24.III.1:1-3, p. 505
356. Text, 25.VI.5:3-5, 8-11, p. 530
357. Fillmore, Charles, *Talks on Truth*, pp. 59-60
358. *Lessons in Truth*, pp. 13-14
359. Fillmore, Myrtle, *How to Let God Help You*, pp. 66-67

Chapter 8: Love and Fear, Sin, Guilt, and Judgment

360. Text, Introduction.1:6-7, p. 1
361. Text, 13.V.1-2, 4-5, p. 247
362. Text, Introduction.1:8, p. 1
363. Text, 13.IV.1:2, p. 245
364. Text, 12.I.9:5-7, p. 217
365. Text, 7.IV.7:7-12, p. 119
366. Text, 7.VI.4:4-7, p. 124
367. Text, 15.V.1:6-7, p. 312
368. Fillmore, Charles, *The Revealing Word*, p. 72
369. Fillmore, Charles and Cora, *Teach Us to Pray*, p. 115
370. *The Revealing Word*, p. 72
371. Wapnick, Kenneth, Ph.D., *Glossary-Index* for *A Course in Miracles*, p. 142
372. Text, 18.I.4:1-2, 3-6, pp. 372-373
373. Text 18.I.5:6, p. 373
374. Text, 18.I.6:1-2, 7, p. 373
375. Workbook, P.I.101.6:7, p. 183

376. Workbook, P.I.101.2:1, p. 182
377. Text, 25.III.9:1-4, 9-10, p. 525
378. Text, 19.III.8:6-7, 9:5, pp. 405-406
379. Text, 22.VI.5:1-2, p. 481
380. *The Revealing Word*, p. 179
381. Fillmore, Charles, *Talks on Truth*, p. 155
382. Fillmore, Charles, *Jesus Christ Heals*, p. 60
383. Ibid, p. 59
384. *The Revealing word*, pp. 179-180
385. *The Revealing Word*, p. 77
386. Fillmore, Charles, *Dynamics for Living*, p.130
387. Fillmore, Charles, *Christian Healing*, p. 90
388. Text, 5.V.2:8-10, p. 84
389. Text, 13.Intro.1:7; 2:1-4, 11;3:1, 5, p. 236
390. Text, 5.V.3:5-6, 4:8-9, p. 84
391. Text, 5.VII, 5:1-5, pp. 89-90
392. Text, 13.II.9:1-3, p. 241
393. Text, 13.IX.5:3-6:8, p. 261
394. Text, 11.IV.4:1-5:1-3, p.201
395. Fillmore, Charles, *Mysteries of John*, p. 17
396. Fillmore, Charles, *Two Undisciplined State of Consciousness*, pp. 11-12
397. Text, 2.VIII.2:3-4, p. 34
398. Text, 4.IV.8:5-8, 10, p. 64
399. Text, 14. III.4:1, 3-4, p. 275
400. Text, 14.V.11:1-3, p. 284
401. Manual for Teachers, 10.2, p. 27
402. Text, 6 .V.C.2:1-4, p. 109
403. Manual for Teachers, 10. 4:5, p. 28
404. Text, 3.I.7:4, p. 38
405. Text, 3.II.2:4, p. 38
406. Text, 14.III.16:1, 4, p. 278
407. Workbook, P.1. Review III. Introduction.6:1-5, pp. 201-202
408. *The Revealing Word*, p. 114

409. *Christian Healing*, p. 121
410. Ibid, p. 121
411. Ibid, p. 121
412. Text, 2.VIII.3:5-7, p. 34
413. Workbook, P.II.10.3:1, p. 455
414. Workbook, P.II.10.5:1-3, p. 455
415. Manual for Teachers, 15.1:11-12; 2:2-7; 3:10-11, pp. 38-39
416. Fillmore, Myrtle, *Myrtle Fillmore's Healing Letters*, p. 130
417. *Christian Healing*, p. 123
418. Fillmore, Charles, *The Twelve Powers*, pp. 43-44
419. Ibid, p. 44

Chapter 9: Healing Consciousness- Establishing Wholeness

420. Text, 11.II.4:1-3, p. 197
421. Text, 10.IV.2:3, p. 187
422. Text, 18.IV.1:1-5, p. 380
423. Text, 18.IV.4:1-2, p. 381
424. Fillmore, Charles, *The Twelve Powers*, p. 151
425. Fillmore, Charles and Cora, *Teach us to Pray*, pp. 67-68
426. Fillmore, Charles, *Jesus Christ Heals*, p. 60
427. Workbook, P.II.1.1:5-7, p. 401.
428. Manual, Clarification of terms, 4.6:1, p. 86
429. Workbook, P.II.1.1:1-7, p. 401
430. Workbook, P.I.122.8:1-5, p. 218
431. Fillmore, Charles, *Dynamics for Living*, p. 143
432. Fillmore, Charles, *The Revealing Word*, p. 77
433. *Dynamics for Living*, p. 246
434. Merriam-Webster, beta, http://www.merriam-webster.com/dictionary/miracle (accessed July 1, 2015)
435. Fillmore, Charles, *Atom Smashing Power of Mind*, p. 38
436. *Jesus Christ Heals*, p. 129
437. Text, 1.I.37:1-2, p. 5

438. Workbook, P.II.13.2.2, p. 473
439. Text, 1.IV.2:3-6, p. 11
440. Workbook, P.II.13.1:1, 3-4, 6, p. 473
441. Text, 27.II.7:1-4, p. 570
442. Text, 28.II.2:8-10; 11:3-4 pp. 593, 595
443. Workbook, P.II.13.2:2, p. 473
444. Fillmore, Charles, *Keep a True Lent*, pp. 178-179
445. *Jesus Christ Heals*, p. 129
446. Fillmore, Charles, *Prosperity*, p. 58
447. Ibid, p. 58
448. Ibid, p. 64
449. *Dynamics for Living*, p. 143
450. Text, 2.II.2:1-4, 6-7, p.19
451. Text, 2.II.1:9-13, p.19
452. Text, 12.I.9:5-10, p. 217
453. Workbook, P.I.34, p. 51
454. Workbook, P.I. 94, p. 164
455. Workbook, P. I.100, p. 180
456. Workbook, P.I.128, p. 233
457. Workbook, P.I.132, p. 242
458. Workbook, P.I.160, p.302
459. Workbook, P.I.187, p. 354
460. Workbook, P.II. 244, p. 415
461. *The Twelve Powers*, p. 150
462. Butterworth, Eric. "You and Your Mind." Unity Magazine 161, November 1981, p 16
463. Cady, Emilie, *Lessons in Truth*. p. 60

CHAPTER 10: CONCEPTS OF THE WORLD AND THE UNIVERSE

464. *Prosperity*, p. 56
465. Fillmore, Charles, *Christian Healing*, pp. 51-52
466. Wapnick, Kenneth, Ph.D., *Glossary-Index for A Course in Miracles*, p. 27

467. Text, 1.III.1:1, p. 8
468. Text, 1.II.3:10-13, p. 7
469. Manual, 18.4:5-6, p. 48
470. Text, 2.VII.6:5-9, p. 33
471. Fillmore, Charles *Talks on Truth*, p. 166
472. Ibid, p. 170
473. Fillmore, Myrtle, *How to Let God Help You*, p. 25
474. Manual, Clarification of Terms 4.1:1-3; 2:3-4, p. 85
475. Text, 21.Intro:1:1-6, p. 445
476. Text, 4.I.4:2-5, pp. 53-4
477. Text, 12.I.10:4-6, p. 218
478. Text, 18.VI.1:1-2, p. 345
479. Text, 12.III.6:6-7, pp. 221-222
480. Text, 18.II.5:1-3, 8, 11-13, p. 376
481. Fillmore, Charles, *Mysteries of Genesis*, p. 41
482. Fillmore, Charles, *The Revealing Word*, p. 162
483. Fillmore, Myrtle, *Myrtle Fillmore's Healing Letters*, pp. 150
484. Fillmore, Charles, *Dynamics for Living*, pp. 121-122
485. Fillmore, Charles, *Keep a True Lent*, p. 89
486. Fillmore, Myrtle, *How to Let God Help You*, p. 25
487. Text, 11.VII.1:1-3, p. 210
488. Workbook, P.I.14.1:2-5, p. 23
489. Text, 13.IX.7:1-3, p. 262
490. Text, 27.VII.11:4-6; 13:1-2, p. 584
491. Manual for Teachers, 14.1:1-5, p. 36
492. Fillmore, Charles, *Jesus Christ Heals*, p. 27
493. Ibid, p. 35
494. Fillmore, Charles, *Talks on Truth*, pp. 163-164
495. *Jesus Christ Heals*, second page of the forward
496. Text, 27.VIII.6:23, 7:2, pp. 586-587
497. Text, 18.I.4:1-5; 5:1-6; 6:2-3, pp. 372-373
498. Text, 13.Intro.2:1-4, p. 236
499. Workbook, P.I.132.4:1-5, 5:1, p. 242
500. Workbook, P.II.3.2:1-5, p. 413

501. Fillmore, Charles, *Atom-Smashing Power of Mind*, p. 93
502. *Mysteries of Genesis*, p. 41
503. Fillmore, Charles, *Two Undisciplined States of Consciousness*, pp. 11-12
504. *Talks on Truth*, p.10
505. Ibid, pp. 30-31
506. Manual for Teachers, 2.3:1, p. 5
507. Text, 1.II.4:1, p.7
508. Text, 1.VI.3:5-6, p. 14
509. Text, 2.II.4:2-4, pp. 19-20
510. Text, 26.V.13:1-4, p. 552
511. Text, 1.1.15:2-4, p.4
512. Text, 5.VI.12:1-5, p. 88
513. *Dynamics for Living*, p. 338
514. *Mysteries of Genesis*, pp. 44-45
515. The Revealing Word, p.195
516. Text, 26.III.2:1-2; 3:1-4, pp. 546-547
517. Text, 11.VII.2:1-4, 6-7; 3:9, p. 210
518. *Keep a True Lent*, pp. 25-26
519. Ibid, p. 102
520. *How to Let God Help You*, p. 48
521. *Mysteries of Genesis*, p. 28
522. Workbook, P.I.183.10:1; 11:1-4, p. 343
523. Text, 11.I.2:3-4; 5:1-5, pp. 194-195
524. Text, 18.VI.1:2-6, p. 384
525. *The Revealing Word*, p. 17
526. *Mysteries of Genesis*, p. 28
527. Ibid, pp. 26-27

CHAPTER 11: THE PHYSICAL BODY, SICKNESS, AND HEALING

528. Text, 6.V.A.2:1-3, p. 105
529. Workbook, P.II.4.2:1-2, p. 419
530. Text, 18.VIII.2:5-6, p. 390

531. Text, 18.VI.9:1-4, 10, pp. 386-387
532. Text, 29.I.8:6, p. 608
533. Text, 2.IV.3:10–11, p. 23
534. Workbook, P.1.136.19:2, p. 260
535. Text, 8.VIII, 3:2-5, pp. 155-156
536. Text, 29.II.7:7-8; 8:1-3, p. 610
537. T-28.VI.5:1, p. 603
538. T-27.I.4:3, p. 566
539. Text, Preface, p. xii
540. Text, 18.VI.5:1, 3, p. 385
541. Text, 8.VII.2:1, 3–4, p. 151
542. Workbook, pI.136.18:1-4, p. 260
543. Text, 8.VII.10:1, p. 153
544. Text, 19.I.2:1-2, 7; 3:1-6, p. 398
545. Text, 28.II.2:8-10; 11:3-4, pp. 593, 595
546. Workbook, P.I.135:9:1-4, 10:1-3, p. 253
547. Text, 25, Introduction, 3:1-2, p. 518
548. Text, 28.11:7, p. 595
549. Workbook, PI.136.15:6-7; 16:1, 4; 17:1-2, 4; 18:1-4, pp. 259-260
550. Fillmore, Charles, *The Revealing Word*, p. 26
551. Fillmore, *Keep a True Lent*, pp. 130-131
552. Fillmore, Charles, *Dynamics for Living*, pp. 332-333
553. *The Revealing Word*, p. 19
554. Ibid, p. 27
555. Ibid, p. 101
556. Ibid, p. 134
557. Ibid, p. 162
558. Ibid, p. 81
559. Fillmore, Myrtle, *How to Let God Help You*, pp. 144-145
560. *Keep a True Lent*, p. 93
561. *The Revealing Word*, p. 136
562. Ibid, p. 173
563. Ibid, p. 92
564. Ibid, p. 77

565. Ibid, p. 28
566. T-2.IV.3:1, p. 23
567. W-pI.96.4:1-5, p. 169
568. T-2.V.1:8-10, p. 25
569. T-2.V.6:3-6, p. 26
570. Fillmore, Charles, *Jesus Christ Heals*, p. 71
571. Butterworth, Eric, *Celebrate Yourself! And Other Inspirational Essays*, p. 55
572. *Jesus Christ Heals*, p. 74
573. *The Revealing Word*, p. 182
574. Fillmore, Charles, *Mysteries of John*, p.124
575. *The Revealing Word*, p. 26

Chapter 12: Unity's Twelve Powers

576. Sikking, Sue. *Beyond a Miracle*. Unity Village, MO: Unity School of Christianity, 1973, p.19
577. Fillmore, Charles, *Keep a True Lent*, p. 165
578. Fillmore, Charles, *Dynamics for Living*, pp. 37-38
579. Fillmore, Charles, *Christian Healing*, p. 107
580. Fillmore, Charles, *The Revealing Word*, p. 35
581. Fillmore, Charles, *Atom-Smashing Power of Mind*, pp. 36-37
582. Fillmore, Charles, *Mysteries of Genesis*, p. 307
583. *Atom-Smashing Power of Mind*, p. 103
584. Ibid, p. 124
585. Fillmore, Myrtle, *How to Let God Help You*, p. 142
586. *The Revealing Word*, pp. 165-166
587. Fillmore, Charles, *Extracts from Letters: Regeneration*, Unity 54:1 (Jan 1921): 59-60.
588. Fillmore, Charles, *The Twelve Powers*, p. 15
589. Adapted from Hasselbeck, Paul and Cher Holton. *Power UP: The Twelve Powers Revisited as Accelerated Abilities*. Durham, NC: Prosperity Publishing House, 2010. p.150

590. Fillmore, Charles. *Releasing the Holy Spirit of God in Man.* Unpublished 3rd lesson, Unity Village, MO, 1931. pp. 4-5
591. *The Twelve Powers of Man*, p. 15
592. Hasselbeck, Paul and Cher Holton, *PowerUP Card Set.* Durham, NC: Prosperity Publishing House, 2009.

Made in United States
Orlando, FL
24 November 2021